∞

*Walking with Jesus
in the Holy Land*

∞

Also available from
Sophia Institute Press
by A. G. Sertillanges:

What Jesus Saw from the Cross

∞

Walking with Jesus
in the Holy Land

by A. G. Sertillanges

SOPHIA INSTITUTE PRESS®
Manchester, New Hampshire

Walking with Jesus in the Holy Land was originally published in French in 1932 under the title *Jésus*. In 1976, Dimension Books, Denville, New Jersey, published an English translation by the Dominican Nuns of Corpus Christi Monastery, Menlo Park, California, under the title *Jesus*. This 1998 edition by Sophia Institute Press uses the 1976 Dimension Books translation, with minor editorial revisions throughout the text.

Jacket design by Lorraine Bilodeau

The cover artwork is a detail of *Entry into Jerusalem*,
by Santi di Tito, Accademia, Florence, Italy
(photo courtesy of Art Resource, New York).

Sophia Institute Press®
Box 5284, Manchester, NH 03108
1-800-888-9344
www.sophiainstitute.com

Imprimatur: G. Lefebvre, Vicar General
Bishop of Paris

Library of Congress Cataloging-in-Publication Data

Sertillanges, A. G. (Antonin Gilbert), 1863-1948.
    [Jésus. English]
    Walking with Jesus in the Holy Land / A.G. Sertillanges.
        p.   cm.
    Originally published: Jesus. Denville, N.J. : Dimension Books,
    1976. English translation by the Nuns of Corpus Christi Monastery.
        ISBN 0-918477-85-9 (pbk. : alk. paper)
        1. Jesus Christ — Biography — Meditations. I. Title.
    BT306.4.S4713   1998
    232.9'01 — dc21
        [B]   98-39097   CIP

98 99 00 01 02 10 9 8 7 6 5 4 3 2 1

∞

Contents

Editor's Note: Except where otherwise noted, the biblical references in the following pages are based on the Douay-Rheims edition of the Old and New Testaments. Where applicable, biblical quotations have been cross-referenced with the differing names and numeration in the Revised Standard Version, using the following symbol: (RSV =).

∞

Foreword

∞

On returning from the land of the Gospels, my heart throb-
bing with fresh inspiration at each step of the way, I have not
been able to resist the natural impulse to which all admiration
is subject, and so I have written this volume.

Much has been written about Christ in our time, some of it
by those who do not know Him or who secretly hate Him. His
holiness and the sacred quality of His life have not always
been approached with a perfect uprightness of soul. There are
some who are not able to bring themselves to acknowledge the
divinity of Jesus, and they are obliged to write about just the
splendors of His human nature. Let God be the judge of these
persons; it is not for us to question their sincerity, even though
some among them appear determined to glorify the man so as
to smother the God under the roses. These people are to be
pitied more than condemned, even when their intentions are
objective in this book. I shall not fail to make use of their particular point of view simply because they abuse it.

Everything about Jesus is admirable, appealing, instructive,
and winning; His soul as well as His life, His actions and the
circumstances surrounding them. But we should not forget
that the man in Jesus is intended to lead us to God; that the
external environment of His human life should not conceal

from us the divine texture; that, in short, Jesus is — by His person of flesh and blood and by His acts — but the nave, as it were, of the temple, the place where the worship begins, but which is consummated on the altar.

∞

*Walking with Jesus
in the Holy Land*

Chapter One
∞

Jesus:
He Lives and Walks
Among Us

∞

The person of Jesus explains His works, and His works receive their true light only from the radiance of His person. Hence it is indispensable for anyone who reads the Gospel to consider what Jesus is by observing what He does.

But how are we to form an opinion of the person of Jesus? By going back to His origins. And what sources reveal His origins? History, as composed by the Gospels and Tradition; authority emanating from Jesus Himself: the Church; and finally the conclusions that may legitimately be drawn, without the least pretension to infallibility from the special conditions of His birth and what Faith teaches us concerning Him.

According to these sources, what do we know?

Jesus was born of a woman. But this woman bears a name that distinguishes her from any other woman. She is the ideal woman, adorned with every beauty, crowned with every grace. So great are her privileges that it would seem that an eternity had been spent to prepare the beauty of her soul.

Mary is a virgin. She is to remain a virgin. God, the principle of all fecundity, including that exercised in His name by all creatures, undertakes to be, in her case, the direct, unique principle of the germination of life. The earth is to bring forth its fruit. But since this fruit is superior to earthly power, while at the same time necessary to its salvation, God reserves to Himself the work to be done, and by His omnipotence, He renders fruitful the womb of Mary.

And what is to be the purpose of this unheard-of cooperation between the Most High and a creature? The formation of a body and soul composing a human nature, and the subsistence of that human nature in a divine person.

That is the unique and unparalleled history of the origins of Jesus. It remains for us to draw from it certain consequences.

The flesh of Jesus proceeds, we have said, from God and from man; from God directly, from man through Mary, a virgin, of the line of David, a quite special creature prepared by God for this work. Insofar as it proceeds from God, the body of Christ should represent perfectly the idea that the Creator formed of human nature. When God acts directly, without the concurrence of created causes (which are always more or less deforming since they are subject to accident), His works are perfect. Why would He aim at imperfection? Or how could it escape from Him inadvertently? It does not become Him to leave any evidence of His passing save what would glorify His wisdom and His power.

This is one of the reasons why philosophers assert that human souls, issuing directly from God concomitantly with the act of generation but superior to it, are all originally equal. The soul of a man of genius and that of the most mentally deficient are not, they believe, at the moment of their creation, in any way different. They are human souls, that is all; equal in species, they are likewise equal in value and in resources. What will determine their differentiation later is the organism to which they are joined and which is subject to the accidents of generation and the effects of heredity; it is moreover the free use that will be made of these, because the soul is formed or deformed by its own action. But all of this is the work of man; on God's part, all is perfect, without any defect or mishap.

In this instance, then, it is God who works; indeed not entirely alone, but as the principal agent, and considering only Him, the creature should be worthy of such paternity.

Jesus proceeds in the second place from Mary and, through Mary, from a magnificent ancestral line. And if it is true that a lineage is like a unique being that is born, develops, grows, and one day attains, through one of its members placed in favorable circumstances, completion and fullness proportionate to the vigor of its beginnings, what must Jesus be in His flesh, even from the standpoint of Mary's collaboration?

The lineage of Mary is that of Abraham, Isaac, and Jacob, the line of David: a lineage at once royal and rural, plunging its roots deep into the bosom of that universal mother, the earth, where all human energies find their source, and growing from age to age under the blessings that came from God on high.

Mary herself, as we have said, is the ideal creature. That she was beautiful all of tradition affirms. All the women who had prefigured her in the Bible were creatures both lovable and strong: Rebecca, Rachel, Judith, and Esther.[1] She herself would symbolize all the charms, all the splendors of virginity;

---

[1] Rebecca and Rachel were the wives of the patriarchs Isaac and Jacob. Judith was the Jewish heroine who delivered her people during the siege of Bethulia; this event is described in the apocryphal book of Judith. Esther was the Jewish queen who saved her people from destruction in the time of Ahasuerus (Xerxes I), King of Persia; the Old Testament book of Esther describes this account.

it would have required very cogent reasons indeed to prevent the beauty of her soul from appearing visibly in her countenance or for her to make use of an enfeebled organism to sustain her supernatural powers.

Under what conditions was she living when the hour for the Word drew nigh? She was dwelling in the temple, the very focal point of the life of her people: an unhappy people who, under the blows of century-old misfortune, was awaiting its Messiah. All the daughters of Judea yearned, with a longing that echoes through Scripture, for the promised maternity. Was it not on this account that sterility was looked upon as so great a curse by every Jewish woman? And was it not for this same reason that virginity was held in such low esteem. It seemed to set a woman deliberately outside the line that might be that of the Christ.

∞

No doubt Mary had higher reasons for remaining a virgin; but she loved her people nonetheless; more than any other did she bear its sorrows; more than any other did she await the salvation of God. She drew it down by her desires; she sacrificed herself to bring it about. Shall we not believe that at the divine hour, at the announcement of the mystery that was to be accomplished, when the angel came to tell her that she would bring forth Him who was to come — shall we not believe that her inmost being was stirred, that the soul of the past and the soul of the future, the soul of the Jewish people and the universal soul of mankind with its accumulated hopes and ardent desires, began to throb in the womb of the Virgin, and that this was the supreme preparation for her sublime maternity?

∞

We think of the body of Christ, then, as endowed with every strength and every refinement. A nature robust and sensitive, entirely free from that effeminacy to which pious imagery is so addicted; the ideal embodiment, the absolute fulfillment of all the desires of the human species, transfigured by a divine alliance: that is what our devotion loves to believe; that is what reason dares to affirm. And what a delight it is to find in the best memorials the confirmation of our expectations. Such is indeed the traditional teaching of the Church with regard to Jesus.

At a certain period, some scholars, without very weighty authority, managed to utter a false note; they went so far as to speak of the *ugliness* of Christ, as if those terms were not mutually contradictory: *ugliness* and *Christ*! They supported their contention (very feebly, to be sure) on the words of the Bible: "I am a worm, and no man,"[2] not recognizing in them a manifest allusion to the voluntary self-abasement of Jesus and to His Passion.

But these represent only negligible differences of opinion against which the Christian soul has always protested, continuing to name its Christ "the fairest of the sons of men,"[3] the preeminent man, the Son of Man, as He called Himself;[4] and the most learned doctors, the Fathers of the Church, have tried to sketch a full portrait of Him that aims at being complete and that possesses the merit of gathering up in a single description the traits scattered throughout primitive traditions.

[2] Ps. 21:7 (RSV = Ps. 22:6).
[3] Ps. 44:3 (RSV = Ps. 45:2).
[4] Matt. 8:20.

Everyone has read such delineations. It would be rash to attach too great an importance to them, of course, but they retain a certain probability; and even probabilities on the subject of Christ are worth a good many certainties about anything else. Gladly do we take the time to seek them out (even the corporeal glorification of the Divine Master).

We love to picture His noble features, His tall figure, His simple bearing, His grave gestures, His serene and compelling brow, that glance in which the soul flashes forth or else conceals itself in the depths of mystery, His mouth delicately molded but firm, exquisitely sensitive yet devoid of all affectation or softness. His whole being is a testimony to His divine and human origins, worthy of His mission among us, capable of expressing to our sight, as His word does to our soul, His sovereign intelligence and His efficacious love.

Theologians recoil from the belief that He ever suffered from our diseases, indispositions, or physical disabilities. All of these, in their opinion, would be contrary to His dignity, the perfection of His body, and the wisdom of His conduct. Incapable of either rashness or lack of foresight, enabled by His most perfect constitution to resist the influences exerted upon us by our environment to which we may not expose ourselves without imprudence, it is inconceivable, they declare, that He should have experienced illness. He had come to suffer; but a nobler, more voluntary type of suffering would seem to become Him better.

Finally, it seems obvious that His features must have suggested the Semitic type; there is no reason to exclude a resemblance that the order of nature indicated. The universal man in Him was not the physical man; moreover that universality was not to cause Him to repudiate His native land — rather, He loved it in a special way. It would seem that He should bear its stamp; and that oriental nature, which impresses its seal so powerfully upon everything, was to retain the glory of forming in its own likeness its divine Son.

∞

Let us penetrate into the sanctuary of Jesus' soul. This is a far greater and more profitable subject. We know it; but do we ever recall sufficiently what constitutes the glory of humanity and the salvation of every man?

What is owing to the soul of Jesus by reason of its origins?

This soul is created by God directly, without the cooperation of any creature. But it is not peculiar in this respect; such is the case with every soul.

It is in fact a little-known doctrine, but one of the highest philosophical significance, that the intervention of God, His direct intervention, is absolutely indispensable for the genesis of each human soul. The generation of man, being a work of the flesh, can result only in flesh; the soul, being a spirit, requires the intervention of God: the Primary Spirit, by whom our spirit is ignited, "as one torch is enkindled by contact with another."

What is there, then, in the soul of Jesus that is proper to it? Its origin is the same as our souls'; can its substance be different? Perhaps not. Substantially, as we have said, in the judgment of a good number of philosophers, all souls are of equal value; they have no *differentiation*; nothing can distinguish one from the other except the special matter that they animate. Since Jesus Christ received from His Father a human

soul, perfectly and truly human, He must be in this respect entirely like us.

But that is not all. The substance of a thing is only the
stock upon which the further developments of its being are
grafted. It is the canvas that is worked upon by God, nature,
and man. What was this work in the case of Jesus? What were
His intelligence, His will? (We leave aside the imagination,
sensitive memory, and the senses — elements that pertain at
once to soul and body, but whose worth corresponds precisely
to that of the organism and which should therefore be as perfect as the human species admits.) What of His intelligence?
God alone knows; we can only stammer about it. Nevertheless, Scripture and Christian theology furnish us with indica-
tions. What do they tell us?

They declare that there must be in Jesus Christ two intel-
lects, since there are two natures. As God, He has the intellect
of God, the knowledge of God, and on that subject we are reduced to silence!

The knowledge of God: any attempt to describe it would be
madness. All that we can say justifiably, without in fact ex-
plaining anything, is that God *is*; that *He alone* is, in a sense,
because everything is through Him, in Him, and belonging to
Him more than to itself. Consequently, God knows all things
because He knows Himself; His universal knowledge is but the
gaze that He casts upon Himself eternally, as upon the common wellspring of all being and all activity.

We admit that this is baffling; theologians, mystics, and all
philosophers who believe in God agree that it must be so. And
the most profound statement, perhaps, that has ever been uttered with regard to this knowledge is not that of a mystic, not

even of a Christian, but of a man who lived four centuries before Jesus Christ: Aristotle.[5] It is therefore the statement of a pagan, which nevertheless brings the thought to greater maturity than all the terrifying declarations of the mystics. In God, he says, the substance of the intellect, the act of the intellect, and the object of the intellect are one and the same thing.

Let us attempt to understand, and we shall have an idea of the divine knowledge of Christ.

What of His human knowledge? It is infinitely below the divine cognition; but if we dare say so, it is even further beyond our powers of analysis. The theologians tell us that He received from Heaven all that was fitting to His personal perfection and His mission. He is the perfect man: consequently He will have all the intellectual perfections reserved to man, both for the present and for the future. First of all, He has strictly human knowledge, which is acquired slowly, bit by bit, through association with other beings and the spontaneous labor of the mind: the first treasure that would suffice to render Jesus greatly superior to every human genius by reason of the transcendence of His mind, manifestly endowed far beyond any other.

In the second place, He has *infused knowledge*, namely, that which is experienced by disembodied souls and by pure spirits, no longer derived from below through sense impressions (since they have no senses, or no longer have them), but from above, from the very source of all that is intelligible. To deprive Jesus of this higher knowledge, which will one day be ours and which has always been that of the angels, would have

---

[5]   Aristotle (384-322 B.C.), Greek philosopher.

meant, according to the Doctors of the Church, rendering Him inferior to His heavenly subjects — something which could not be. Through this knowledge, Jesus knows all that it has pleased God to enable His creatures to know and far beyond that, no doubt, in order to ensure the supereminence of Christ.

Finally, the knowledge that the theologians term *beatific*, because from it will emanate those inebriations of spirit promised to us as a reward, that knowledge which is drawn directly from the vision of God by an unparalleled act that causes us to contemplate face-to-face and as if by sight the Infinite Being: that is the crown of the intellectual edifice in the Divine Master.

To contemplate in its source all that was and all that is, all that will be and all that might be; to penetrate with His gaze ever more deeply into the powers of God; to discover in God all the plenitudes of being, all the forms of truth, all the shadings of beauty, and all the degrees of harmony, life, and existence under all its aspects, in an inebriation of spirit that was constantly increasing in the measure wherein He penetrated further into this infinite: such was His destiny. Just as a cloud pierced by the sun's rays becomes dazzling with light, says Bossuet,[6] so it is with the soul exposed to God. In proportion to its penetration of Him, the soul is also penetrated so as to become like God by gazing on the divinity.

That, in the judgment of Catholic theologians, is what the human perfection of Christ demands.

---

[6] Jacques Bénigne Bossuet (1627-1704), French preacher and Bishop of Meaux.

∞

Moreover, even if He were not entitled to all this on account of propriety, we should still find the reason, theologians declare, in the exigencies of His mission. Jesus Christ is not only the perfect man; He is the universal man. Upon Him rests the salvation of the world. His knowledge must therefore give Him competence and power over all the domains wherein His action is exerted, over all the details that He must govern.

Even if our world, small indeed, is but an "out-of-the-way corner of nature," as Pascal[7] calls it; even if the stars that wheel about us should be populated beyond measure, what they contain could not be unknown to Christ. The glory that He draws from His personal union with the divinity is necessarily as universal as God Himself, and it would be absolutely impossible for His knowledge not to extend to the *all* — whatever that might be, to the all of time and the all of space — or that, extending to the whole, it should not penetrate into the very last detail, as the knowledge of the Ruler of the worlds extends to the least hair of our heads and to the number of sparrows on the rooftops.[8]

Here we cannot avoid a thought that presents itself irresistibly in the face of this Omniscience, a consoling thought, to be sure, but one that arouses astonishment bordering upon stupor: How could Jesus Christ, knowing all — all that we are, all that we are worth in terms of misery and wickedness, and

---

[7] Blaise Pascal (1623-1662), French theologian, mathematician, and savant.

[8] Cf. Matt. 10:29-30.

what this earth, upon which He had just set His divine foot-prints, amounts to — fulfill unto the end what He had come to do?

Are there not unfathomable abysses in that very thought?

As for those who say, "Christ is a wonderful man, an ideal man; but He is only a man": all this is understandable in the face of the great mystery of Christ. They will tell you, "He tried to elevate humanity because He was mistaken in its regard. He believed in it; He hoped to raise it out of the mire; but He died in the attempt, and He died disillusioned." That is clear — as clear as it is blasphemous!

But there are those who say, "He knew everything. He saw the whole future: all the mysteries of evil; all the shady underside of souls; all the accumulation of centuries of iniquity; all the concoctions of that Devil's kitchen of sin which is the world. He saw all that. He saw the radiant sun of His heavenly Father lighting up the crimes of humanity, carrying off at eventide its harvest of dark deeds and, with the dawn, garnering the shameful legacy of night. He saw that, yet did not recoil in horror before His task. He saw what could be expected of a faithful Christian in His service and of a scoundrel in His dishonor; and neither such affront nor such homage was able to arouse His utter disgust. He saw us all, and He said, *'Peace be to you!'* "[9]

Anyone who considers this mystery will be overwhelmed by it, and he will only be restored to tranquillity so that he may savor with delight the incalculable mercy, the forgiveness beyond all reason, the pity as vast and untroubled as the

[9] John 20:19.

firmament, the goodness that is capable of reconciling for all men these two attributes: supreme understanding and supreme love.

∞

It remains for us to analyze the will of Christ. We need not dwell upon it at length after what has already been said; for the will follows the intelligence.

The will is only the weight of a being drawn toward an object that the intelligence finds desirable; it uses its various resources for the purpose of achieving it.

Jesus, having a divine intelligence, must have had a divine will, that is to say, an infinite love of the good and, in the service of that love, omnipotence itself. Since He had in addition a human intelligence with all its perfections, He must have had a human will with all its resources: self-possession in truth; the orientation of self and all its endowments toward the supreme good, which is God; absolute impeccability in His life; infinity of merit; certain efficacy in His prayer; and assurance of success in all His works, which He undertook only in conformity with the will of God and as the instrument of His strength. But let us not belabor the point; all of this is self-evident.

As we have remarked, in the service of Christ's intelligence, there were His admirable secondary faculties, such as the imagination, the sensible memory, and the senses; likewise, as we must acknowledge, below His will and in its service were those redoubtable but necessary energies of ours that we call the *passions*.

We should not be intimidated by that word, *passion*. If human misery often condemns it to a connotation of weakness, it nevertheless possesses of itself a very noble meaning: it merely signifies the sense reaction aroused in us by an object, whether contrary or congenial.

Hence there were passions in Christ. Love, hatred, desire, sadness, hope, fear, and even anger found a place in His human heart. But that which in us is often a blind or inimical force, riveting us to the earth and destroying the power of grace, was in Jesus a lever of the soul in the service of good. As a matter of fact, it was these passions that, while furnishing the material for merit, made of His life the divine drama, capable, in the judgment of twenty centuries, of fascinating the minds and hearts of even His enemies.

There is the analysis, one might say; but what of the synthesis? How can all of that hold together? How is the divine being compatible with a human nature and faculties? How can infinite knowledge tolerate in the same being the proximity of an inferior knowledge, let alone of three such types of knowledge: *infused* knowledge, *beatific* knowledge, and *human* knowledge? Even considering only the human intelligence of Christ, how, in that intelligence, could *infused* knowledge, complete from the beginning since it came from on high, and *beatific* knowledge, also complete and infinitely higher since it has God for its immediate object, endure the coexistence of a progressive knowledge, one that was slow in developing, since it had to wait upon the work of the senses and consequently upon opportunity and age to furnish it with the materials of progress? Then, if the same problems are posed with regard to the volitional faculty and all the others, and if we are urged to clarify these castles of the soul wherein our intellect becomes altogether lost, we shall have but one answer in reply: mystery. That is always the last word.

We could write a great deal on the subject, and in fact people do. It is not too difficult to dispel the contradiction that attempts to bar the way of dogma; but that does not dispel the mystery. So why linger over it?

God is God, and we are nothing. God knows all, and we are ignorant and blind. God can do all, even things of which our childish knowledge knows nothing. And is it not to be expected that Christ, who represents for us the highest degree in the scale of beings, should also present to us the profoundest mysteries?

The lowest form of being, the mineral, is a mystery. And on this first mystery of inorganic matter is grafted the greater mystery of life, such as we find it in plants. The animal adds to it the mystery of sensation. And man adds still further the mystery of thought: mystery upon mystery, even in this purely human order. Finally, in Christ, it is the mystery of the infinite that comes to complete and crown all the others. Is it astonishing that this should baffle us beyond measure, so that we can say only, "O God, Thou knowest all, and Thou canst do all things"?

Let us put a halt to this brief study. Its only pretension is to recall what must be true about Jesus Christ before observing Him at work.

At any rate, the Christian likes to recall that, if the divine riches of Jesus Christ remain inaccessible for us, we are invited to share in all the treasures of His humanity, body and soul. However, Jesus possessed the most precious of His glories even in this world; in our case, it is elsewhere that we are to participate in them.

The glorification of the body, glory of soul, eternal youth, infinite splendors, ineffable peace, tranquil possession of immense benefits, and rapture of the entire being in the inebriation of power and the ecstasy of love: that is our lot; that is our hope. The condition for it is that our life should be conformed to that of Christ insofar as human weakness allows.

If He came into the regions of this world, it was to open new worlds for us and to show us the way.

Chapter Two

Bethlehem: He Enters Our World Quietly

Of all the aspects of Jesus' life, the most charming, the most intimate, and the sweetest, in the judgment of Christian peoples, is that which we are reminded of, amid a long procession of memories, by that magical, soft name of *Bethlehem*.

The whole life of the Master seems to be contained in a few words. After Bethlehem there will be Nazareth, the lake,[10] and Jerusalem. Nazareth signifies mystery; the lake stands for labors; Jerusalem means strife. And all of that combined is life each day with its activity, its aspirations. Bethlehem is the morning. It is the freshness of dawn, the first smile of daybreak; it is a pure, faint breath lifting the soul into an azure sky, filling it with mysterious fragrance, such as those that pervade our dreams when we muse on the blissful paradise where the first man reveled free from care.

Bethlehem! There is a festal air in the very sound. It awakens a host of distant cadences, like the song of angels and the flutter of wings. As soon as we pronounce it in our hearts, the imagination chimes in with the peal of Christmas bells and all the joyous reminiscences of childhood. At the same time, reason finds in it profound and serious lessons.

[10] The Lake of Gennesaret, also known as the Sea of Galilee.

∞

God had decided upon the propitious hour to fulfill the hopes of His people. He had not fixed His glance upon the great, the powers that be, the religious or political chiefs; He had selected from a poor little hamlet a child of lowly circumstances whose name was *Miriam:* Mary.

Much like one of those still seen on the way that leads to the fountain at Nazareth — serious of mien, draped in the traditional costume that was long ago that of the women of Isaiah's time: a tunic of multicolored stripes wherein the blue predominates, a white veil, a cincture of soft stuff lightly twisted; steadying with one arm her full pitcher while with the other she draws her veil about her — such was God's choice.

To this girl of scarcely fifteen years, while she prayed in her dark chamber hollowed out of the rock, God had sent an emissary: one of those beings whose superior nature does not hinder them from fraternizing with the little race of human creatures, for the glory of their common Father. The angel had presented His request, and consent having been given, the mystery was accomplished. Heaven had bowed down and had charged the earth with hope by filling the womb with hiddenness and the heart with love.

Some months later, an edict of Caesar Augustus[11] arrived. A census was to be taken of the whole country; there was a journey to be made. Mary's husband, Joseph, the spouse without guile, was of the family of David; hence Bethlehem, the city of David, was his as well. To it he must go to be inscribed.

[11] Caesar Augustus (63 B.C. - A.D. 14), Roman emperor from 27 B.C.-A.D. 14.

It was an ill-chosen moment: Mary's time was approaching.[12] But the pride of emperors is not accustomed to consider the trials it inflicts; and so they set off on the way. It was a matter of four or five days' travel. They departed, equipped probably like one of those groups to be seen at every turn along the roads of Palestine: the Virgin mounted on an ass; Joseph walking at her side with his staff and, over his shoulder, together with his coat, some provisions for the journey.

The route they would take would be the one they followed three times a year at the great feasts: the plain of Esdrelon, Naplouse, and Jerusalem. Each evening, they made a halt at one of the caravansaries always open to travelers on the outskirts of towns and villages. This was a century-old establishment; beasts and men took shelter there, generally in the neighborhood of a well, and in the morning, with no one to thank save God, they set off on their way.

Often the pilgrims who thronged this road as the feast days drew near would sing psalms in honor of that Zion toward which they were journeying. Perhaps the souls of Mary and Joseph were too full for such outward expression; but if their lips were silent, the *Magnificat*[13] made melody within them with every modulation of joy and love.

They reached Jerusalem, skirted its western walls close by the citadel, traversed the plain and the hills that would soon echo with the cries of Rachel's grief,[14] and in two hours arrived at the little city of David. We may well take the time to

[12] Luke 2:1, 4-5.
[13] Luke 1:46-55.
[14] Cf. Matt. 2:16-18; Jer. 31:15.

describe that countryside out of which Bethlehem rises, in the midst of bare hillsides, like a clump of greenery out of the rocks.

A stone's throw from Jerusalem, the ghastly city beleaguered by the desert on the east and scarred with deep wounds by the Cedron and the hideous Gehenna,[15] Bethlehem sits charmingly upon its two hillocks. Its amphitheater crowns the hollow of a valley that is a veritable horn of plenty. Hence it was formerly called Ephrata,[16] "the fruitful." The industry of its inhabitants had planted abundantly in broad strips set upon circular terraces like steps, with fig trees and climbing vines that even today trace their graceful pattern upon the white soil.

Bethlehem was a favorite stopping place for Solomon.[17] He had gardens planted there that extended below the town into the little Ortas valley. Above, close to the Hebron road, he had constructed immense basins that still exist. They were filled by the waters of a delightful spring hidden in the depths of a subterranean grotto known as the Sealed Fountain, just as the valley itself was called the Enclosed Garden, with reference to the poetic names given by Solomon to his bride in the Canticles.[18]

---

[15] Gehenna was the Valley of Hinnom, southwest of Jerusalem (Josh. 15:8), known as the site of human sacrifices to Molech (cf. 4 Kings 23:10; RSV = 2 Kings 23:10). In the New Testament, the name Gehenna refers to Hell (cf. Matt. 5:29).

[16] Mic. 5:2.

[17] Solomon was the son of David and king of Israel from about 970 B.C.

[18] Cant. 4:12 (RSV = Song of Sol. 4:12).

It was these basins to which we have just alluded that sup-
plied, by means of conduits at ground level, the buildings of the
temple and the holy city; the life of Jerusalem had its source
there, just as the life of the world issued from Bethlehem.

∞

Even today, Bethlehem is charming. When we have as-
cended the little hill and emerged upon the typically oriental
small town square, which is the center of Bethlehem's life and
faces the sacred grotto, covered over by the most ancient basil-
ica in the world; when our eyes have scanned the white slabs
of a cemetery bordering the crest of the hillsides and the fresh
green of the tiered gardens, down into the valley of the carob
trees where they vanish, and onto the little mound that bears
the village of Beit-Sahour somewhat beyond, the one from
which the shepherds came, the threshing-floor of Boaz and
the field where Ruth the Moabite woman gleaned,[19] then we
see on the horizon, at the right, the Dead Sea and, at the left,
Jerusalem, the city of blood. And when finally, side by side
with these memories, attractive and sinister by turns, we observe in the square, moving about among the rows of camels
crouching under their burdens, young girls in long, white
veils, sisters to the Virgin, and children in striped gowns, like
the sons of Jacob, gracious in their own right but even more
wistfully so when we recall their little brothers, the Holy Innocents,[20] and their other brother, Jesus: all of this produces an

[19] Ruth 2:3.

[20] The Holy Innocents were the children of Bethlehem who
were murdered by King Herod's order, in his attempt to
destroy the Infant Jesus (Matt. 2:16-18).

indefinable atmosphere in the soul. A strange and deep feeling seizes the soul: it is a kaleidoscope of thoughts at once melancholy and sweet, the focal point of which is a cradle announced by ominous forebodings and subsequently fashioned into a Cross.

But if we linger in these places until nightfall, even more intense impressions are aroused. For to us Bethlehem means *the* night; it means midnight; silence on the horizon; nature calm and undisturbed; the lovely rising slope of the hillside, under the gentle pulsation of the stars, reaching upward to draw the Beloved out of Heaven. When, in the presence of the reality that fulfills what we have dreamed, we wait for the coming of eventide, seated against one of those tombs — so white as to recall the swaddling-bands of Jesus, thus clothing their melancholy with an indefinable charm — and having watched the fantastic symphony of sunset, inebriating and lovely as the glory of Heaven, we see the darkness mounting, gradually climbing higher, hovering above our heads, noiselessly switching on its constellations, while from below arise, in gusts of sultry air, the sounds of flocks scattered here and there in the distance, as if the plain itself were murmuring or the night exhaling the ghost of a sigh: then the combined effect grips the heart, exquisitely torments it. And should we at that moment, by simply turning our heads, declare to ourselves, "There is the place!" — what an exalted, intoxicating experience we would offer our imagination.

For the time being, the present no longer exists; in a faraway dream world we seem to hear indistinct voices from the past which, without articulating anything distinctly, convey very much. Then we are quite prepared to see the holy couple coming forth upon that square, weary from their long journey, but filled with great interior peace and joy.

∽

It was toward evening that Mary and Joseph must have arrived at their journey's destination. They had been preceded there by a certain number of their compatriots, travelers like them coming from various points in Judea; hence it was very natural, in so small a town as Bethlehem, that there should no longer be any room for them in the caravansary.

We are all familiar with the beautiful moral applications inspired by this fact in the Fathers of the Church. In their eyes, this crowded public inn is the human soul. There is room for many things in our lives. Like those shelters provided by oriental towns, which are wide open to every newcomer, we, too, are open to whatever appears attractive or pleasing. The mob enters in; it invades us, absorbs us. A host of thoughts, desires, earthly preoccupations, affairs, and passions: all of this finds room. But when Jesus presents Himself, He has come too late.

At times we are afraid of such a guest. He is embarrassing, this Jesus Christ! Wherever He enters, He demands plenty of room — room that is undisputed and commanding. How can He be lodged side by side with certain other guests we have admitted? And so we say, "Be off with You!" We do not actually utter the words with our lips; but the heart is more eloquent than the mouth, and our heart says to Him, "Go away! There is no room. Leave me in peace. Be off with you!" And He does go. And we remain in our wretchedness, like that caravansary of Bethlehem, which might have received the Infinite under its roof, but refused to do so.

So there are Mary and Joseph without a lodging, wandering through the streets of Bethlehem, urged on by the fall of night and by the time — which is drawing nigh. It is not difficult to imagine Joseph's anxiety; who can describe his earnestness and his distress? It was so unexpected, this reception, and so cruel.

As for Mary, the touching preparations mothers make for the birth of their babies should give us some idea of how it must have hurt her. Yet not even the shadow of anxiety could skim the surface of her soul. She bore within her the Ordainer of all things, Him who knows all, who can do all. To be worried in His regard would have been childish. As for herself, what did it matter to her? Did she not possess all things, having such a treasure? When she considered the lot that had been given her, could she envy mothers who were wealthy or comfortable? To suffer, with Jesus under her heart, was a twofold joy to her: it meant sharing the role of the Savior before He entered upon it Himself; it meant carrying the Cross, while carrying Him who would be stretched upon it.

The secondary redemptrix of humanity was now beginning her heavy task, with what an immensity of tenderness every Christian heart will understand as long as it knows how Mary was associated in the great work of Christ and, consequently, how much she was to participate in the universal joy she was bringing.

So she went through the winding lanes of Bethlehem without fear, without anxiety. She was waiting upon the will of God; and God poured into her soul, drop by drop, His tranquillity, greater far than that of the night rising from the plain and slowly enveloping the lovely slope of the hill. Meanwhile the ineffable exchange went on: Mary giving to Jesus her blood, her life, the pulsations of her heart; Jesus giving to Mary light, strength, love, patience, and the peace of one possessing God.

Guided by her spouse, guided even more by Providence, seated upon her poor mount, whose hoofbeats resounded on the stone doorsteps like a summons forever unheeded, Mary went along in silence, Heaven hidden beneath her lowered eyelids, shrouding with her veil the heart where God reposed. Meanwhile Joseph anxiously sought shelter everywhere; but he found nothing.

Finally, no longer expecting anything from men, they thought of those shelters that never close their doors to the poor. Under the slope of the hill, in the neighborhood of David's tower, there were a certain number of caves such as one frequently sees in Palestine, especially in Judea. They were used as cattle sheds; but since the flocks were led to pasture in that season of the year, they happened to be unoccupied. It was in this direction that Joseph and Mary turned.

Providence was leading their steps. God willed for His Son no other shelter than those which He Himself prepares for His pensioners. Maternal and industrious, this motherly Providence supplies a lodging for every living creature; it hollows out caverns in the depths of the forests; it forgets not even the whelps of the lioness, as Holy Scripture observes.[21] When in past eons it presided over the vast transformations of the material universe, when fire was shaping the molten mass of this globe, it preserved this rocky cave, in anticipation of the divine hour.

[21] Cf. Job 38:39.

It did not become Immensity to confine Himself within a man-made dwelling. It was not fitting that He — supreme in opulence, commanding the extravagant outlay of each day's dawn, setting the brow of night with dazzling jewels, casting about the shoulders of a crumbling wall a brilliant mantle richer than those of kings — should be born surrounded by our tawdry treasures. He dominates them by eschewing them. He shows His greatness by choosing what we call wretchedness. He wills no other luxury than what befits the restorer as well as the founder of the earth. The flower of this world — and not a hothouse flower — He wills to blossom in the midst of creation, with no other architect or interior decorator for His birthplace than the God whose Son and equal He is.

Moreover, is it not fitting that He who is the man of all men should, from His very first hour, be accessible to all, especially to those who resemble Him the most: the humble, the lowly, the despised, whom He loves? Look at those shepherds skirting the edge of the Judean wilderness, a black veil covering their heads, a sheepskin thrown over one shoulder, a threadbare tunic gathered close at the waist, and a short club cut from the sycamore tree in hand, to hurl after the wandering sheep. These are the men to whom Jesus owes Himself. They are nothing — less than nothing; especially in the Orient, they are the servants of servants and, like Jesus, they have no other shelter than the overhanging rocks. It is to them first of all that Jesus would offer Himself.[22]

These shepherds are nearby, guarding their flocks in the plain. They drowse or chat among themselves around their

---

[22] Luke 2:8-12.

campfires, which they do not yet recognize as beacons, and silently Jesus invites them. In a moment, they will come, and, without ceremony, without any fear, since shepherds and kings have equal rights, they can gaze upon, love, adore, and — if they dare — take into their arms this Son of God, in the simplicity and peace of their hearts.

Is it for this that Heaven impels the travelers toward the cave? There is no temple yet for the Real Presence; but nature is the vast temple opening to her God. Behold its dome: this rock. There is the manger for an altar. The holy couple, Mary and Joseph, have entered. The moment approaches upon which Heaven waits. Mary trembles with expectant hope. The dark lodging, made habitable by Joseph's solicitude, offers its humble resources to the hidden God. Then Mary's holy spouse withdraws. Confident of mysteries, he retreats into his nothingness before the face of the Infinite who is coming. And then, all of a sudden, here God is, resting in the cleft of the rock.

Under its shadowy veils, Bethlehem sleeps. Nature slumbers, too. The stars look down, quivering gently. The angels, attentive, ready to burst into their hymn of joy, wait upon the signal in the eyes of their Master. Everything is in readiness, and the mystery is accomplished.

Chapter Three

Nazareth: He Exalts Our Daily Life

∞

Anyone who might have penetrated the soul of Jesus would have discovered in Him, even in the excitement of His active life, hidden depths full of silence where His interior life expanded at a profound level and whose external action was but a delicate veil.

But what characterizes its beginning — thirty years of obscure and apparently useless existence — is an inwardness, an aloofness, a silence of unbelievable proportion. Concerning Nazareth, the Gospel is silent; in Nazareth all is mystery and quietude. Like Moses in the cloud, conversing with God alone, so it is with Jesus. Is it rash to attempt to draw aside its curtain?

∞

At the time of Jesus, Nazareth was a small hamlet lost amid the hills of that Galilee which all scholars and experts held in contempt. "Can anything good come out of Nazareth?"[23] they asked rhetorically.

It was, in fact, a place of no importance. Three or four thousand inhabitants, a synagogue with perhaps a small school

---

[23] John 1:46.

37

annexed to it: that was all. There was no center of trade; no
Roman garrison; none of those country estates that filled such
towns as Tiberias or Magdala with bustle and, it must be admitted, with corruption. Still less could Nazareth boast of one
of those famous institutions of learning such as the court of the
temple sheltered, and which constituted the glory of a Jewish
city.

Situated some sixty miles from Jerusalem, nine hours on
foot from Capernaum, far from the high roads, Nazareth was of
no consequence. It waited. It was that rose of which St.
Jerome[24] speaks, opening its calyx for Heaven alone.

Today the pilgrim who goes up from Jerusalem discovers
the little white town sheltered like a swallow's nest among the
hilltops that dominate the Plain of Esdrelon. Approached
from the north, however, from Upper Galilee, it appears to be
in a hollow. That is because it lies hidden in one of those tiny
mountain valleys scooped out in countless numbers between
the snowcapped ridges of Palestine.

When you reach the place, your mind a prey to the great
remembrance, your soul filled with the thought of the Savior
and His unfathomable childhood, barely touched upon in a
few vague phrases of the Gospel; when you consider what He
was, what He is, the awesome mysteries that His soul contains,
the eternities through which His life develops, the immensities wherein His name resounds and His works unfold: then
you are overcome with amazement!

Look at this village, its flat-roofed houses like scattered
blocks of stone amid the vegetation; the street that climbs

---

[24] St. Jerome (c. 342-420), biblical scholar.

along the ravine it has hollowed out for itself, which must be as old as the countryside, along which the whole life of the little town ebbs and flows and settles down. There it is! That is Nazareth! This is the hidden life: thirty years of an existence whose every minute saves the world. *My God, how small are Thy immensities!*

The mind, disconcerted for an instant, suddenly feels delightfully shaken by the impact of these overwhelming memories together with such familiar scenes. Is this where Jesus lived? Was the world's priceless treasure deposited here? And did He spend thirty years hidden away from men — like this tiny hamlet between the hills, lowly amid the lowly, exposed to rebuffs, to commonplace associations — earning His livelihood by plying a trade? Yes indeed!

Jesus Christ had not come upon earth for His own sake; He came for ours. To suffer and to be humiliated on our account; to be humiliated and to die for us: that was His destiny; and Nazareth is only a stage on the way to Calvary. And because this is so, it is a wonderful source of encouragement for those who have their Calvary to bear here below.

The lowly, the little people, those who find their lot in this world to be nothing but wretchedness and obscurity, can say to themselves: He was poor; He was lowly as I am and for love of me. And this humility shared by two becomes sweeter, and progress along the way becomes easier, when the end of my cross rests on the shoulder of God.

∽

May we not also consider that what was humiliating for Jesus as man was a higher source of pride for Jesus as God?

Walking with Jesus in the Holy Land

What difference do our human conditions make to God? Our pretensions, our positions, our superior advantages: what does He care about such things? Poor little gnats, strutting about, despising other gnats because their wings are a little less sleek and their feet not quite so thickly furred: of what consequence is all that to Him? Whether we are great or small, in His eyes our conditions are equal, and since no one of them corresponds to His nature, did not His honor demand that He should choose the lowest? Only thus could He manifest His indifference. By identifying Himself with the negation of our glories, He would show that He is sufficient unto Himself. One can hardly imagine how, in the presence of Nazareth, these thoughts assert themselves. The human condition of the Savior becomes so apparent there that the divine point of view is dazzlingly clear. And this poverty, freely chosen, draws in its wake, before the mind's eye, the eternal magnificence. And this nothingness is the best pedestal from which we can leap upward toward the infinite.

Now we have entered into this Nazareth; we have followed the narrow streets as far as the house — can we call it a house? — where the Infant-God lived in silence. It is a recess below the rock that formerly may have possessed a little fore-part constructed of masonry. Nowadays it is a chapel to which people come to pray, kneeling under its dark vault. Every priest may bring down God in that spot, thus renewing two thousand years later the Real Presence. What a great number of thoughts occurred to me there: how the past rises out of the very ground, starts from the walls themselves, while Heaven seems to bend down, to gaze intently and lovingly over this mysterious corner of the world.

They lived here. They loved the shadow of this rock. Peacefully, in this spot, they led the life of these poor folk whom we have seen so often in the villages of the East, hidden in the depths of their miserable dwellings, far removed from our civilization, from the complications of our seeking after comfort, but close to nature and close to God.

Mary was there. She went twice daily to that well — the very same one from which no one can draw water without walking over the wet ground. Barefoot and modest, she advanced single-file among her companions; she set down her jar, awaiting her turn, which was often long in coming on account of the congestion of the single town well; then she returned home carrying her burden. She set her poor little house in order, bearing the Infinite in her heart. She kindled a fire in one of those recesses dug out of the earth that are the only chimneys of the Orient, and then she prepared food for the sovereign Lord of all things! She baked the bread earned by Joseph and Jesus. And the angels above looked on with wonder over this purest of creatures.

We reflect on how deserving of pity they are whom so much humility scandalizes, who go away saying to themselves, "Is that all!" Yes, it's true: that is all! The Creator of the heavens is troubled by no such false shame. All is great from the viewpoint of Him before whom everything is small; and since His heart inclines Him to abase Himself, He is exquisitely happy and proud to abase Himself lower and still lower.

∞

How should we look upon those thirty years spent in the obscurity of Nazareth? It was a time of preparation. Jesus Christ had no need of preparation on His own account; the problem of vocation, so difficult for others and settled more or less tardily, was determined beforehand in His case. From the very first minute, conscious of Himself, He knew what He wanted; He could bring it about if He so willed, but it did not please Him to do so. He awaited the hour of men. His divine authority must have as its visible support His human authority; He awaited that human hour, patiently permitting His life to unfold and His moment to come.

Does this mean that those thirty years were devoid of results from the standpoint of the divine plan? To believe this, one would have to be profoundly ignorant of what He is.

Jesus Christ came into the world to give Himself, to say a word, to offer an example, and to die. Death would come in its time; it is too early for the word; but there remain the example and the gift of self: the example of humility, of patience, of submission to God and to His representatives on earth; the gift of self — to whom? First of all, to His Father.

Let it be clearly understood that this act, basically, is the real function of Christ. Is He not a ransom? Is He not the price of the guilty and the intermediary for the just? The voice crying out, "Behold I come, O God, to do Thy will"[25] — is it not the whole Redemption, the whole priesthood of Christ, and consequently, His entire work?

The rest is an excess, a marvelous excess of love, of condescension, and of justice. But the essential is there. In the simple cry "Behold me!" the whole Redemption is condensed. But that cry represents Jesus Christ entirely and at every moment,

---

[25] Cf. Ps. 39:8-9 (RSV = Ps. 40:7-8).

in Nazareth as well as on the Cross. John the Baptist used to say to those sent to him from Jerusalem, "I am the voice of one crying in the desert."[26] Jesus Christ is the *Voice* calling out to God. All that He is and all that He can do, all His thoughts, all His feelings, all His aspirations, all His joys, all His sorrows, every sigh from His lips, and every beat of His heart: all of this cries out to God; all of it supplicates, pleads, intercedes, and makes reparation; all of it, issuing from a divine Person, possesses a divine value; and the world is saved by looking on its Savior.

In this way, by giving Himself to God, Jesus Christ also gave Himself to men. In that charming, recollected Galilean temple, in that dwelling permeated with silence, where silence was the very atmosphere and they no doubt spoke only in the praise and service of God, He presented to the world the real presence.

Like the winter sun, serenely radiant, rising over the slumbering white landscape, which apparently neither warms nor fructifies, but seems to have come only for the sake of shining and rejoicing the heart: so was Jesus. Hence, when one visits those places, they seem like a sanctuary. The hillsides are altars; the trees, the flowers, the rocks, and the filmy clouds, like sublime adornments for that repository to which Heaven bowed down. Between these objects and those that are merely profane, there is all the difference that our imagination discovers between the shrubs that decorate a tabernacle and the same shrubs lying dusty along the roads. Indeed Nazareth is a temple. It is the holy ark bearing the living law of the Most

[26] John 1:23.

High;[27] it is the golden candlestick shedding light over the world;[28] it is the rock whence poured the living water to flood the earth and purify it.[29]

∞

What did Jesus do at Nazareth? The Gospel answers: "Jesus grew in age and wisdom and grace before God and man." And it adds the words: "He was subject to them."[30]

One could hardly express with more profound simplicity the fact that at Nazareth Jesus was in no way distinguished from His companions in Nazareth. He wanted His actions to resemble ours so that our merit might resemble His.

As a child, He played on the ground with those who would later be referred to as "the brothers of Jesus,"[31] that is to say, His maternal cousins and other children of the town. No doubt they played as children do today — for the East changes little, and moreover, the Gospel suggests this — at weddings and funerals or else with tame birds, a favorite sport of young Orientals. These childhood games form a part of the picture of that glory filled with grace of which St. John speaks in his Prologue.[32]

When He grew older, He had ordinary dealings with everyone, distinguished only by the perfection of His life, to such an

---

[27] Deut. 10:5.

[28] 2 Paralip. 13:11 (RSV = 2 Chron. 13:11).

[29] Cf. Exod. 17:6.

[30] Luke 1:52, 51.

[31] Cf. Matt. 12:46, 13:55; Mark 3:31; Luke 8:19.

[32] John 1:14.

extent that even His cousins didn't know! This will be seen later in their opposition as well as their complaints.[33] The glory of an hour at the divine cradle had been so discreet that nothing remained of it afterward. A veil of silence had been spread over the Beloved; faith alone, under the glimmering light of sweet memories, taught even Mary and Joseph what their Child really was in truth.

Of course, they must have prayed together. Like all Jews, they pleaded for the redemption of Israel. And then what feelings stirred in that sacred group! What union of hearts! What glances! What a mysterious fear on the part of some! What discreet abandonment on the part of the other! Jesus was silent about Himself, and His silence was understood. These were divine hours, hours they must have wished would never end.

But life was waiting; they must act; and the days passed by, spent, except for the hours of ritual worship, partly in study and partly in labor.

∞

Study is a strange term applied to Jesus. Yet, remember: we have acknowledged in Him, beside what is of God, all that pertains to man; consequently, an intelligence capable of development, at least with regard to the manner of learning that depends upon experience and the spontaneous activity of the mind. Human science in its perfect stage was no more due to the Child Jesus than the figure of a grown man to His body or a steady gait to His walk. Strictly speaking, He learned nothing from man, but He learned from things and from Scripture,

---

[33] Cf. John 7:3-5.

which He must have loved to scan, for He found in it the name of His Father everywhere. All of this was taken for granted.

From the age of five, every Jewish child was expected to begin learning verses from the Bible. At ten years of age, he was initiated into the rabbinical traditions later compiled under the name of the *Mishnah*. On the Sabbath and feast days, the long hours of leisure spent at home were given over to this responsibility. In addition, a great number of towns had a little school attached to their synagogues. Each master was in charge of twenty-five children; he taught them by the question-and-answer method, as the Divine Master Himself was later to do so often. He instructed them in reading from small rolls of papyrus or parchment; then he taught them to transcribe with a *calam*, or reed, using the beautiful characters of the sacred language, the passages from the Bible that it was deemed wise to have them learn, such as the story of creation, the feast-day hymns, and the articles of the Law. Finally this summary instruction was completed by practical lessons on the manner of conducting oneself in the various circumstances of life, a kind of course in etiquette and correct social usage for young Orientals.

Thus did Jesus spend His first twelve years. At that stage, a new path opened up before him; it was the age marked out for initiation into social life. He was admitted by right into the privileges of worship. For the first time, He would be going up to Jerusalem.

∞

Jerusalem: it is not difficult to imagine the emotion that took possession of the heart of Jesus as He passed through its gates and walked into the temple for the first time. The appearance of that famous edifice, the plan of which had been designed by God Himself, in which His Law was kept, through which His praises had echoed for centuries amid the confused clamor of idolatrous cults; the sacrifices, symbolic of His own, pouring out torrents of the victims' blood, amid the smoke of incense and the rising tide of prayers: this was enough to stir to the very depths that heart so easily moved to pity, so easily inflamed by anything that touched the honor of the Father.

At the moment when the Levites and sons of Levites intoned the Psalms, after the great Paschal libation, historians tell us that it was like a voice of thunder that shook the foundations of the temple and rolled off even into the valley of Cedron. Jesus must have joined His voice to that concert of homage and, sending back to the Father the echo of His own voice, repeated with the psalm, "Behold I come, O God, to do Thy will."

We should not stress too much the episode that marks this first visit to the temple. Jesus in the midst of the doctors is only a portent; this is the downpayment of the wisdom that we shall see opening its treasures. The daring words of Mary, "Son, why hast Thou done so to us?"[34] are a striking commentary on those other words: "He was subject to them." Finally, the Savior's reply — "Did you not know that I must be about my Father's business?"[35] — sums up His whole life. There it is completely, just as the whole essence of light is present in a sudden flash of lightning.

[34] Luke 2:48.
[35] Luke 2:49.

But His hour has not yet come. The star will withdraw into the night, until it rises resplendent over the world. Let us return to the Holy Family in Nazareth to consider another spectacle, that of Jesus the worker.

From His childhood until the days of His public life, Jesus labored. It was a necessity, for Joseph's household was poor. There was a duty involved from which the Son of Man should not excuse Himself. An Israelite who did not teach his son a craft was looked upon with scorn. "It is as bad as encouraging him to be a brigand," said the rabbis. Even the masters of sacred doctrine worked with their hands. Hillel was a wood-carver, Shammai a carpenter;[36] there were some who were not ashamed to ply the trade of shoemaker, tailor, blacksmith, or potter. The practical, hard-working spirit of the Jewish race has never given this up throughout the centuries.

Moreover, it was particularly becoming that He should labor who had "not come to be ministered unto, but to minister,"[37] and who wished at one and the same time to sanctify work and to sweeten its burden by offering us an example.

Work is a virtue and at the same time the seed of virtue, for it banishes from us the suggestions of evil; it keeps our powers of body and soul vigorous; it brings us close to our fellowmen; it benefits social conditions far more than the idle theorists or the lazy rich who complain about the misfortunes of our day and do not wake up to the fact that they themselves are a social plague, an object of envy and scandal to their brothers, a

---

[36] Hillel and Shammai were influential rabbinical teachers of the time of Christ.

[37] Matt. 20:28; Mark 10:45.

deadlock in the great living organism, a clot in the stream of human life. Thanks be to God, the greater number are not such.

Labor is the ordinary condition of mankind. That is why Jesus, who has a duty toward everyone, gave people this striking example: a Christ who was a worker during the greater part of His life.

What kind of work did Jesus do? Tradition is unanimous in declaring that He worked in wood. It is easy to picture Him at work in one of those little rock-hewn carpenter shops common to the Arab section of Nazareth. The men work not far above the floor, where the shadow meets the light, bare-armed and bare-legged, cutting out yokes and plows, one foot poised to hold the wood in position; or else skillfully turning the little rails to form a latticework with a strange primitive tool known as a bow, under which the tiny splinters flash in the sun like a shower of pale gold.

We can imagine Jesus working in the same way — only more recollected, more modest, more silent — and is not the picture one of sublime dignity? The contrast between these lowly occupations and Him who deigns to engage in them gives the spectacle a solemnity that can only be called religious. In spite of ourselves, we become more thoughtful, drawn by an inward summons to unite in thought with the stream of ideas that filled that silence, the ineffable purposes that motivated that labor. Self is forgotten in silent contemplation of the divine workman calmly laboring in a shadowy corner. The eye follows His hands, seeks out His glance, sees His soul filling with its serene radiance the little booth, and Nazareth, and the world.

Walking with Jesus in the Holy Land

∞

It can be conjectured that the labor in which Jesus engaged was not always very intense. The attitude of His people and of His era did not lend itself to it. It would be a mistake to imagine in an Eastern workshop the feverish pace that prevails in one of ours. Our more severe climate has created lively competition; our energy is exerted with a kind of frenzy for the satisfaction of more-or-less artificial needs. But the East is not like that. Even today, but more especially then, life is patriarchal and tranquil. Labor has its place there, no doubt; but it gives way to leisure that is prolonged, thanks to the simple life the people lead.

∞

On the Sabbath and feast days, moreover, work was always suspended. What did Jesus do then?

We have already suggested that He prayed, He read the Bible, and He contemplated. On the flat roof of His oriental-style house, or on some promontory in the neighborhood, He would settle Himself down to read or pray or think. How many times, perhaps, did He not scale one of the summits overlooking Nazareth, whence He could view the whole terrain, all the roadways of His future Apostles.

To the north are the Lebanon and Anti-Lebanon ranges, with Hermon capped in snow. On the east is the Sea of Galilee, scarcely concealed by a screen of hills, the future setting for divine exploits. To the south, Gelboe, the peaks of Ender, Gesrael, and further off, Ebal and Gerizim, together with the plain of Esdrelon, reminded Him of the great wars and noble deeds of His ancestors. Quite close at hand, Tabor presented Him with the pedestal for His glory. Finally, in the west behind the whitening summits of Carmel, the "Great Sea,"[38] over which the good tidings would take their flight with outspread wings.

It is not difficult to guess what transpired there in the soul of the Master. When in the evening the horizon narrowed under the deepening shade of nightfall; when He watched, on the level stretches about Him, the winnowers with their wooden scoops casting the seed into the summer breeze, the laborers returning home, the flocks raising little clouds of dust in the distance, and the night watchmen arriving for their turn to keep vigil; when the fragrance of almond and lemon blossoms rising from the depressions between the hills reached the height of His vantage point: surely His reverie must have been sweet indeed. His imagination was peopled with those lovely images that He would give to the world in His parables. And in all, this charming natural beauty, on the earth as well as at the edge of Heaven, Jesus read the name of His Father, discerning the sublime symbols that radiate and veil His truth.

Later, when immersed in action to the utmost, He would make it a rule to safeguard His solitude. He is given to the world, but in what measure His wisdom determines. He is seen, He acts, speaks, cures, consoles, exhorts, and becomes all things to all men; but when that is accomplished, His interior life asserts its rights and He withdraws into solitude. "He went into a mountain alone to pray," the Evangelists tell us several

[38] The Sea of Galilee.

times.[39] For whole days and even several days, they seek Him without finding Him. It was the desert or the mountain fastness that attracted Him. He would be off in some shady retreat, at the foot of one of those mighty trees or in a cave such as one finds everywhere in Palestine from which He could glimpse the sky, and there His soul mounted up to God.

Obviously, let us repeat, that soul carried its solitude about everywhere, even in the midst of bustle and noise; but He sought out visible withdrawal for the instruction of His followers and for us. We, too, must learn to recollect ourselves. Whatever our cares may be, we must form for ourselves an interior life where the worries of our occupations shall not enter except to give greater impetus to the life of the soul.

Exterior works are well and good, but on the condition that they spring from an inner depth that gives them value in the eyes of the Master. What do our works amount to of themselves? What does it matter to God to have our hands or our brains working? And whether others gather the fruits, or we ourselves, of what worth are these fruits unless they lead to eternal life; what will remain of them tomorrow, when we and those who belong to us have passed on, and the balance sheet of life is settled in the coinage of the soul? We must therefore cultivate our soul; to do so, solitude and recollection are necessary. Solitude invites God, opens the heart to great thoughts, enables us to reach our innermost being, where strong resolves are conceived and our real resources lie concealed.

That is why the hidden life is a great example: thirty years, as compared with three years; three years of action and thirty

---

[39] Cf. Matt. 14:23; Mark 6:46; Luke 6:12.

years of silence, of insignificant labors, of hidden devotedness, and of obedience. It was obedience to God, to His representatives, to the events He controls; detachment from self and from what He would later call "the world,"[40] that is to say, evil, false maxims, false appearances, and false loves: that was then the whole glory of Christ. It would have to be ours, too.

Our life is not brilliant every day; in large measure, it is a hidden life. To impregnate it with the spirit of Christ is to fill it with peace, to give it divine serenity, the assurance of being secure in our way, with a glimpse of the reward at the end, which is Heaven.

[40] Cf. John 15:18-19.

Chapter Four
∞

Palestine:
He Preaches in Words
We Can Hear

∞

Nazareth is a preparation. Work was on its threshold. The moment was at hand when Jesus, who had come to restore humanity, would labor to accomplish this great undertaking. He would have to recall the truth to men's minds, and therefore teach. He would have to struggle against the empire of sin, and therefore exhort. He would have to reunite men to God by a bond of love, and therefore reveal that love to them, enable them to know the heavenly Father, and inspire them with confidence in His bounty.

The public life of the Savior had this triple object. That is why Joseph's carpenter shop was left empty one day and the Son of Man showed Himself.

Under what conditions the transition from the hidden to the public life was made is revealed by the Gospel. Jesus first went to the Jordan River, there to be baptized by John the Baptist.[41] He who was instituting Baptism wished to be the first to give an example of it. He wished to sanctify, by His contact with it, that water which was to serve for the regeneration of His children. He desired to wash, in His pure flesh, the stained flesh of the sons of Adam.

[41] Matt. 3:13; Mark 1:9; Luke 3:21.

Walking with Jesus in the Holy Land

So He went from Nazareth, cutting off to the east toward the very bottom of that enormous depression into which the Jordan rushes on its way from the north, and where, thirteen hundred feet below the level of the Mediterranean, the Dead Sea sinks as into a grave. There He received the testimony of John, the testimony of the heavenly Father;[42] He went down into the waters of that river which, flowing through Palestine from end to end, produces life as Jesus was to produce it for the world. Then He went back toward the solitudes surrounding Jericho, wishing to live alone for forty days[43] and thus enter upon His active life through the avenues of silence.

These solitudes were the ones into which the seers of Israel formerly came to retemper their souls, and where the precursor, exhausted with fasting and haunted by messianic visions, poured forth his prolonged supplications after having preached and baptized all day along the river bank. At the moment for beginning His work, Jesus withdrew to this desert as if to make more intimate contact with the Father, to plan with greater calm His years of labor. He also fasted and endured the assaults of Satan, who had taken it upon himself to thwart Him in His purpose.[44] And turning toward the future, He took in at a glance the work to be done. Like the sun, in the psalm, "He rejoiced in spirit to run His course";[45] like a giant, on fire to reveal His soul, rich with the treasures of infinity, and to pour it into the soul of the masses.

[42] Matt. 3:16-17; Mark 1:10-11; Luke 3:21-22.

[43] Matt. 4:1-2; Mark 1:13; Luke 4:1-2.

[44] Matt. 4:1-11; Mark 1:13; Luke 4:1-13.

[45] Cf. Ps. 18:6 (RSV = Ps. 19:5).

After forty days, He returned to the banks of the Jordan and, mingling with the crowds that hastened from all parts to hear the preaching of John, He spoke.

Three questions present themselves to us with reference to His message: What was its setting? How was it put forward? What are its dominant characteristics?

∞

The setting for Jesus' apostolate is the tiny region hemmed in on the north by Lebanon, on the east by the hills of Moab and Gilead, on the south by the Dead Sea and the desert, and on the west by the Great Sea. It was an area about equal to that of Switzerland; a hundred and fifty miles long, according to St. Jerome's calculations. As to its width — scarcely fifty miles — this great Doctor found it so unimpressive that he dared not mention it, lest, as he writes, he might seem to provide ammunition for the blasphemous sarcasm of the pagans.

As a matter of fact, there is something strange, almost disturbing, in the thought that the immensity of Jesus' life was entirely encompassed by such a space. Two days' journey traverses the country of Jesus from end to end! And it is of Him that Scripture says, "It is a small thing that thou shouldst be my servant to raise up the tribes of Jacob and to convert the dregs of Israel. Behold, I have given thee to be the light of the Gentiles, that thou mayst be my salvation even to the farthest part of the earth."[46] What a contrast between the vastness of that mission and the apparent restriction of this field of action. When the brethren of Jesus said to Him, "If Thou dost

---

[46] Isa. 49:6.

these things, manifest Thyself to the world,"[47] one is tempted to say that they were right. How could Jesus, the universal man, consent to spend His life at what appears to be marking time, making contact with the universe at only a single point?

Instead of the scandal that some take at this, it seems to us that it manifests one of the divine characteristics in the conduct of the Master. God has a liking for this procedure which consists in causing immensity to spring out of nothingness, a great tree from a tiny seed. He Himself created out of nothing so that nothingness might render testimony to His power; and just as He constructed nature, He also constructed supernature.

He could have sent His Christ to all the shores of the universe; He could have prolonged His life until it encompassed the life of the world. He preferred to reduce to a minimum both that life and its setting. Thirty-three years, or rather just three years, is certainly a minimum for an active life. Palestine is indeed the minimum for a fatherland. Considering times and places as a whole, they do not count for much; and it is precisely because they do not count that God preferred them. His Christ would not go beyond this little Judea. He cares nothing to go beyond this patch of land. He walks the length and breadth of the tiny domain, taking months to make a four-day journey, and when He shall have said a word and given an example, He will die, leaving to His Apostles the responsibility of conquering the universe.

The Apostles: do we ever think of the rash folly, were it not for the omnipotence of God, of entrusting them — *them!* — with the conquest of the world? A few boatmen, a collector

[47] John 7:4.

of customs: that is what they were; poor fellows He had snatched from their jobs one day and who often had no idea what He was talking about. He knew them so well. He knew they could not be counted on, and forbade them to rely on themselves. But He added, "I will send you my Spirit."[48] It is this Spirit which would renew the face of the earth.[49] It is the presence *in spirit* of Jesus Christ that matters for His work, and not His corporeal presence:[50] that is why He acts without agitation and dies without fear. Men are in a rush because they are not masters of time; they want to accomplish everything themselves because they are not masters of other people: they cannot confer upon them genius or anything that might take its place. But Jesus Christ is master of time and master of men. His earthly life is only a lightning flash; His earthly country is a mere point; but from that point of space and time with which His mortal condition is linked, His influence radiates over all space and all time.

Would it not be accurate to restrict even further the theater of Jesus' apostolate, and say that the real Gospel country is that Galilee on the shore of the lake, which every Christian soul looks upon as a fatherland and which is even more impressive than Jerusalem? When the pilgrim approaches it by way of a long caravan trek, he seems to be walking backward into history. Each step erases still more time and, when he reaches the shore, transported twenty centuries into the past, he seems to have become for a brief hour the contemporary of Jesus.

[48] Cf. John 15:26.
[49] Ps. 103:30 (RSV = 104:30).
[50] Cf. John 6:64 (RSV = John 6:63).

In fact, this is where the new law was proclaimed. Seated upon an outcropping of rock, surrounded by a crowd ranged in tiers upon the slopes and narrow terraces that overlooked the lake, Jesus spoke, opening the human heart to Heaven.

At that time, about ten towns dotted the little inland sea. How often He went from one to another, crossing these waters, now placid, now storm-tossed, on the way to Capernaum, which they called His hometown, to Bethsaida, Chorazin, Magdala, or wherever there was a soul to be harvested, the seed of a word to be sown.

Today silence reigns over these waters. Desolation inhabits the shoreline. It would seem as if no reality dares encroach upon that dream: the presence of a God. Scarcely a few signs of life: a boat, a few fishermen dragging in their nets as in the days of Andrew and Simon Peter, a nomad's tent, with the natural charm of these beaches imposing its melancholy note everywhere — that is all. The whole takes on a ghostly aspect, as of living symbols that appear to have no other reason for existence save only to give some foundation to a dream.

The fact is that one can scarcely approach these regions with ordinary sentiments. In this perfectly authentic site, so delightfully motionless, where the silence of adoration seems to brood, where the clamorous life of former times has become set as in a smile, where nature celebrates a perpetual anniversary, each year silently donning her festive garb, bringing out flowers by the valleyful, charging the drowsy air with fragrance and color, shot through with quivering sunlight: in such a setting, the imagination is roused and stimulated. It is inebriated with the past, and the regenerated centuries speak to it. One seems to hear pulsating in the atmosphere, resounding yet mysterious as an interior voice, the whole Gospel of Jesus: "Blessed are the poor! Blessed are they who mourn! Come to me, and I will refresh you!"[51] It reverberates from across the wall of centuries, and one cannot help remarking, "At this very hour, from all the corners of human habitation, the throngs of souls who read the Gospel converge upon this spot, which I have the privilege of treading upon; their dream hovers mistily above the wave over which my boat glides; I sense their breath and that of the souls of all ages who have dwelt in spirit beside these waters."

There comes to mind a day on the heights of Gadara, a little hill commanding the lake from a distance of two miles or so. Seated upon a rock that formed a kind of promontory, I watched one of those magnificent sunsets which are the constantly repeated glory of Eastern skies. The orb descended slowly, as if ensconced upon the violet haze rising from the shore. The lake spread out beneath it, while, radiant and mellow, it flooded the water's surface with its placid glow. And high above, its aureola melted into the firmament, stretching out to right and left to skim the crest of the hills until it met the distant horizon which looked to the human eye like the very edge of the world. And I whispered to myself, "Behold the Christ!"

He spent His life confined within this small domain. Like the sun, which seems at this moment to belong to the lake, coming so close to it, seeming to have an eye for nothing else, and yet illuminating the world and living in the heavens, so was Jesus. He trod this soil; He climbed this Tabor which I saw

[51] Cf. Matt. 5:3, 5, 11:28.

before me; He spoke and acted in the midst of an infinitesimally small group. But actually, His message was addressed to the world; His action was worldwide. What difference does it make on which spot of ground He set His feet? The setting is negligible; the reality enacted is infinite, and it is to all men that Jesus addresses what He said to the fishermen on these shores and to the meager crowds who followed Him.

How did the Savior proceed in His preaching? We would expect to see Him, as lawgiver and teacher, appearing with a code of laws in hand, a complete body of doctrine embracing all the grand objectives He proposes. But he offers nothing of the kind: no text, no system, and nothing organized or presented according to any order whatsoever. He presents Himself, and it is He who is the doctrine and the truth. He permits Himself to be seen, and that is already teaching; He acts, and that is teaching; He speaks, and the teaching becomes more precise, but without being fitted into the adapted framework of a system. His message exposes itself to the apparent chance of circumstances; and it is the ordinary environment of Jewish life that will be that of His apostolate.

Every Sabbath, in all sizable towns, the people gathered in the synagogue; they prayed together; they read the Scriptures, on which some notable member of the congregation was invited to give a commentary. Jesus availed Himself of this custom, and a passage in St. Luke graphically describes what then occurred.

It was the Sabbath day in Nazareth. Jesus, invested "in the power of the Spirit," entered the synagogue "according to His custom."[52] After the usual prayers, the people were waiting for a reading from the Book of God when, from the midst of the assembly, a young man arose indicating that He wished to speak. It was Jesus the carpenter. Great must have been everyone's surprise. No one is a prophet in his own country, as the Savior was to say later.[53] What they knew best about Him in Nazareth, in spite of the rumor that must have already reached that place concerning His apostolate, was that He had never studied under any master and scarcely knew anything but the use of His tools.

However, the leader of the synagogue acquiesced. Jesus mounted the ambo, a kind of platform with wooden lattice-work on which the Bibles were spread out, and, receiving from the hands of the *hasan* the book of the Prophets, He began to unroll the bands, and read: "The Spirit of the Lord is upon me because He has anointed me to bring good news to the poor. He has sent me to proclaim to the captives release and sight to the blind; to set at liberty the oppressed; to proclaim the acceptable year of the Lord, and the day of recompense."[54]

Then He stopped, closed the book, returned it to the *hasan*, and seated Himself for the commentary. Every eye was upon Him, St. Luke tells us. They were waiting for what He would say. And amid the silence, He began: "Today, this Scripture has been fulfilled in your hearing!" With sublime eloquence, He presented to them the idea that through Him the kingdom of evil was about to end. And all bore witness to

[52] Luke 4:14, 16.

[53] Cf. Luke 4:24.

[54] Cf. Luke 4:18-19; Isa. 61:1 (Revised Standard Version).

Him, the sacred writer tells us; they marveled at the words of grace that came from His mouth. And they said, "Is not this Joseph's son?"[55]

More frequently, at other times, Jesus went about the country, speaking and healing on His way, entering the villages, stopping with groups, waiting for souls beside the wells, or walking up and down under the arcade of Solomon's porch at Jerusalem, surrounded by disciples; or else, in Galilee, gathering the crowds at the edge of the lake, climbing onto a rock or into a boat Himself, so as to rise above them, and letting His heart follow divine inspiration.

By every means and with reference to everything, the questions He is asked, the events that occur, the cures He performs, the tributes He receives, the opposition He encounters, the conversions He effects: He speaks; He casts the seed; He diffuses His thought, His sentiments, and all that He is. It is truth that rests, as in its focal point, under its human sheathing, luminously visible in response to every appeal.

What was true of His scene of action is therefore also true of the preaching itself. Jesus was not anxious to go everywhere; nor did He make a point of saying all there was to say, much less of saying it systematically. What has He to do with methods and systems? Why should He wish to express all things in one lump?

He is living authority, dispensing truth in proportion to the demands of circumstances. And that authority, showing itself manifestly for only a moment, eclipsing itself, so it would seem, at the Ascension, in reality remains indefectible. "Behold I am

[55] Luke 4:20-22 (Revised Standard Version).

with you . . . unto the consummation of the world,"[56] said the Savior.

Let it be understood: it is the society He founded, the Church, which is His living authority. Continuator of His mission and acting under His eye, teaching in His name, She, too, with reference to the various incidents in the lives of peoples, formulates what is to be believed and what is to be practiced. In this lies a great difficulty for our separated brethren of Protestantism who worship the Gospel and reject the living authority, not perceiving that the Gospel is only one fragment of Jesus Christ, and that Jesus Christ whole and entire lives in the Church.

Everything is consistent in the work of God. The achievement of Jesus Christ overflows the narrow confines in which it seems to be enclosed; a wisdom and a serenity that can only be divine preside over the organization of that plan which includes the whole life of the world: it is a vast snare, entirely the work of love, in which the universe is to be caught.

The characteristics that distinguish the preaching of Jesus can be reduced to two: simplicity in depth and persuasive power resulting from the supernatural certitude of the speaker, of His character, and of His life.

The qualities of simplicity and depth cannot be separated in the words of the Master. He brought the wisdom of God; He came to illuminate human life, to reunite it to its principle, which is the Infinite, and to orient it toward its end, which is a

---

[56] Matt. 28:20.

supernatural end. He Himself, Jesus Christ, was a living mystery; and it was essential that He should make Himself known. In any case, His language could not help but be profound.

On the other hand, He was addressing Himself to simple people. In contrast to the Pharisees who made contempt for the lowly and ignorant a principle of their conduct, almost of their virtue, and in contrast to the men of genius who claimed to reform human thought, and hence addressed the upper classes while setting aside or neglecting the common folk, Jesus was and remains the man of the people.

He offered as a sign of the divinity of His mission the evangelization of the poor; it was essential that the poor should understand. The groups that gathered about Him — among whom the most prominent personages were Peter the fisherman and Matthew the tax collector of Capernaum — would not have followed Him for long had He presented them with learned abstractions. It was necessary that the infinity of God should accommodate itself to the weakness of these men. That is what He did.

Read His discourses. All of them — with the exception of some special and very rare occasions — are of a simplicity that can only be termed regal; that word seems to describe their character accurately. Royal personages, within an intimate circle, speak of great affairs with disconcerting simplicity. Kingdoms, scepters, and crowns are looked upon by them as commonplace objects are by us. Thus Jesus speaks with calm majesty about the divine things He offers us. His eloquence is naturally sublime because its subject matter is naturally divine. For this reason, it is simple, spontaneous, natural, and without artificial outbursts or sensational or feverish effects.

Read the prophets with reference to the same subjects: the difference is striking. The prophets are agitated, for their inspiration comes from without. They are *ravished* to the point of being beside themselves; they follow the intermittent, tempestuous flights of the Spirit into regions of light that are beyond them. But Jesus bears the light within Him: it radiates from Him quite naturally. He has no need of leaping forth into realms of mystery; the mystery is in Him; the mystery is Himself, and He reveals it by opening His hand.

One quality, however, was called for. If this message was to capture the people, it must be graphic and vital.

People are like children; as a matter of fact, all crowds are like children in this respect. They must be spoken to in imagery, comparisons, and figures of speech. The Oriental is particularly fond of pointed witticisms and vivid expressions. The rabbis of the time were well aware of this: the Talmud is filled with such expressions. Jesus, for His part, avoided abuses of them and preserved what was of value. His is the witty sally, the vivid picture, the telling remark, the superb yet homely comparison.

He rejects the fable, which contains an element of falsity and childishness out of keeping with divine thoughts. But He adopts the *parable*, a transparent veil with ample folds, beneath which truth at once reveals and bedecks itself; an admirable stimulant for the mind, the imagination, and the senses, in which an actual occurrence, delightful or touching, trenchant or serious, assists us in accepting its uncompromising conclusions.

And these parables are not outlandishly drawn from the distant realms of fantasy or caprice; Jesus took them from real life, everyday scenes, and objects near at hand: mountains, towns, springs of water, sepulchers. He gathered them as He passed by, from the wheatfields where the wildflower hides,[57] from the pastures where white sheep and black goats, separated into two flocks, suggest to Him the picture of the judgment,[58] from the vineyards protected by watchtowers, such as the heavenly Father planted,[59] and from the orchards where the barren fig tree encumbers the ground.[60] All nature rose up in some way and hastened to enter into the wondrous framework of His message, just as the palm branches along the road to Egypt bowed down, according to the legend, offering Him the tribute of their fruits.

When He happened to be in the temple at the moment of the great ritual libation, He called out, "If anyone thirsts, let him come to me and drink."[61] When they lighted the great, sixty-foot branched candlestick in the court of the temple, which illuminated the whole city, He said, "I am the light of the world."[62] If it happened that He saw the flocks destined for the sacrifices, coming from the Judean wilderness to the temple through what was called the Sheep Gate, His comment was, "I am the door of the sheep. . . . No one comes to the Father but through me."[63]

---

[57] Cf. Matt. 6:28.

[58] Cf. Matt. 25:31-32.

[59] Cf. Matt. 21:33; Mark 12:1.

[60] Luke 13:7.

[61] John 7:37.

[62] John 8:12.

[63] Cf. John 10:7, 14:6.

The people, entranced by His words, cried out, "No man has ever spoken as this man speaks!"[64] And they forgot everything else in their desire to hear Him. "The multitude was in admiration,"[65] the Gospel keeps repeating over and over. When He asked them, "Have you understood all these things?" they exclaimed, "Yes, yes!"[66] Then, casting, as it were, a net over that mass of souls, He uttered one of those declarations, as simple as nature itself and as expansive as infinity, to terminate His discourse: "Truly, I say to you, this generation will not pass away until all these things take place. Heaven and earth will pass away, but my words will not pass away."[67] Thus did He speak at the end of one of His familiar instructions.

Into what splendor the simplicity of the divine speech is transmuted! What a vision! What an immense prospect! How it evokes, with a simple word, the myriads of ages required, perhaps, to measure cosmic disturbances. Unheard-of transformations, tremendous cataclysms, collapsing worlds that, so the Psalms tell us,[68] God changes as we do our coat: that is what it conjures up. And His word, He tells us, immutable amid the shifting sands of the world, will never pass away; it will soar above the rise and fall of eons like a sublime and ineradicable law.

Regarding the authority of the Master's word, we have but one observation to make, and it will not be difficult to guess

[64] Cf. John 7:46.
[65] Cf. Luke 5:26.
[66] Cf. Matt. 13:51.
[67] Matt. 24:34-35 (Revised Standard Version).
[68] Cf. Ps. 17, 28, 96 (RSV = Ps. 18, 29, 97).

whence it proceeds. His word was filled with power, the Gospel tells us, and He was teaching them as one having authority, and not as the scribes. Indeed, yes! He was the first, the only one having authority to teach men. Who, in fact, has power to teach men? Truth — Truth alone. He who is not the Truth but puts forth his personal authority either deceives others or is self-deceived. But Jesus Christ is Truth; He is substantial Truth. That is why He appealed to so few. He speaks, and He demands belief in His word. He teaches as God must have taught the first man, proceeding by affirmation and with a serenity which derives in Him from the sense of truth and produces this sense in others.

No discussion: "Amen, amen, I say to you"[69] — does that not suffice, considering who is speaking? His calm certainty sets His doctrine infinitely above human disputes, in the inaccessible regions of eternity. By means of a maxim, a parable, or one of those clear, incisive flashes that enlighten the intelligence with a single stroke, He meets every situation, disentangles the thorniest problems, replies to the most wily of sophists, crumbles to bits a fabric of arguments like a glass spear that dissolves into dust when the point is broken. Even His enemies are reduced to silence or to words of approval: " 'Thou hast spoken well, Master.' And no one after that ventured to ask Him questions."[70]

That was because He who spoke was not a mere orator. He had within Him the certitude of God; and He also had the power of God. He could emphasize each of His statements

[69] John 1:51, 3:3.
[70] Cf. Luke 20:39-40.

with a miracle. A miracle proves the veracity of one's teaching as the thunderclap proves that there has been a flash of
lightning.

Even from the human standpoint, He had all the qualities
that enable the truth to make its mark. He had disinterested-
ness, an exclusive concern for the designs of His Father, and a
true love for the common people, whom so many others flatter
in order to exploit them, but whom He reclaims, corrects, consoles, and cures, like a firm, benevolent father.

He had personal charm, an ideal combination of every
noble attraction, of all the graces. Above all, He had His life,
consummately pure, supremely charitable, and perfect beyond
human powers. Confronted by His enemies who objected to
His doctrine, He looked them in the face and asked, "Which
of you shall convict me of sin?" and this truly divine challenge
was answered by nothing but silence. He had a right to conclude, "Why, then, do you not believe me?"[71] His life testified
in His behalf and repudiated every suspicion of error or deceit.
He was holy, holiness in person; hence He was true — Truth
itself. These two elements are inseparable.

Happy the times that heard such things! Blessed the regions that gathered up their fragrance! All these memories,
and more, are awakened as we travel through this land, now
the abode of silence. Everything recalls some detail, a sacred
incident, a parable of His. We advance reverently, as in a temple or along a triumphal way. This earth that supported Jesus,
this lovely sky that covered Him, these hills that hearkened to
His voice, the enduring look of things that struck His eyes: all

---

[71] John 8:46.

of this moves the soul delightfully and plunges it into a most touching reverie, impelling us to read and reread the Gospel narrative.

But why do we read it so sparingly?

Chapter Five
∽

In Solitude:
He Teaches Us
to Pray

∞

For Jesus Christ, as we have said in reference to Nazareth, external life is a secondary matter. His real work is a hidden one, consisting of His invisible relations with God and with creation. Nor is there anything surprising in this: we are not far from being in the same position ourselves. What are words and actions, on the basis of which men judge us? They are the surface of our life and, as it were, a kind of thin crust. Underneath lies the soul. All that interior world of thoughts, desires, inclinations, aspirations, dreams, joys, and sorrows is what makes us basically what we are. In order for others to know us, it is not our words that must be understood; it is our silence. It is not our actions, but our repose; it is that interior life that goes on in obscurity, almost imperceptibly, beneath the surface activities, just as in the depths of the sea, far from the surface calm or tempest, there swarms and surges a whole world of living beings.

In Jesus Christ, the contrast is far deeper. As we were saying, the stage of His external action was insignificant; likewise, the duration of that action was insignificant. Of what use would it have been of itself, then, had that been all? We all know that this was by no means so.

Jesus Christ acts outwardly for our instruction; but it is within that the real drama is performed. That is where the great issue is dealt with, between the heavenly Father and the Man-God. All of this comes to light in His prayer. That Jesus prayed cannot be doubted; the Gospel declares it time and time again. What may indeed puzzle us is the explanation of this fact, which, at first thought, seems unreasonable. Jesus is God; as such, can we conceive of His uttering a prayer? As man, He is so close to the divinity by intelligence and will that we cannot see what prayer could add to this, or what means might still be left to the lifting up of His soul for bringing it about.

Nonetheless, Jesus' intellect, insofar as it resembled ours — by which we mean that act which renders us the slave of an object at the precise moment when it holds us captive — was able to seek its deliverance and, at certain times, concern itself with God alone. Moreover, the bond existing between Him and His Father must be manifested; and nothing could succeed better in doing so than the fact of their intimate relations in prayer. Finally, Jesus owed us an example. He obeyed without having to obey, suffered without being obliged to suffer; died without owing anything to death; and He willed to pray in order to teach us "always to pray."[72]

It is clear that Jesus prayed above all in the situations indicated by the Jewish law: at the synagogue, as we have said; at the temple, where the worship of God, scrupulously carried out, included many prayers. Notably, every evening, at the end of the day's ritual, a libation was poured out, and, accompanied by the temple musicians, the Levites intoned the Psalms. Each psalm was divided into three sections; at each

[72] Luke 18:1.

interval, the priests blew three blasts on their silver trumpets. That was a signal for the people to adore.

Nothing was omitted that might command respect. The adorer was to mount the steps solemnly and in silence. He was to carry in his hand neither staff nor sandals nor wallet nor bag. It would seem that these very recommendations, later addressed to the disciples when they were setting off on a preaching tour,[73] were intended in the mind of the Savior to inspire them with the consideration that their ministry was a real form of worship, comparable to that of the temple.

As the attitude of prayer, there was the bowing of the head, the bending of the knee, and the prostration, such as our Lord made use of during the prayer of His agony.[74] The adorer, when he had risen up, was to assume a proper bearing, with his garments well arranged, his feet together, his eyes downcast, his hands folded on his breast, standing before God, as the rabbis said, "like a slave before his master with the greatest reverence and fear."

It is not hard to imagine the Savior, modest, grave, praying with earnest intensity there in what He called His Father's house. He practiced the Jewish ritual before supplanting it; He burned the last incense before the altar would crumble to dust.

∞

In the second place, Jesus prayed with His Apostles. The words that He was to leave us, "Wherever two or three are

[73] Matt. 10:9-10; Mark 6:8; Luke 9:3.
[74] Matt. 26:39; Mark 14:35; Luke 22:41.

gathered in my name, I am in the midst of them,"[75] He must often have fulfilled literally. Sometimes with the whole apostolic group, sometimes with but two or three, as on Tabor,[76] He set the tone of the prayer; He encouraged His followers by example.

One day this scene took on a special grandeur and solemnity. It was on the Mount of Olives. After the turbulent days spent in the temple precincts disputing with the doctors, Jesus would retire there with His intimates. Seeking retirement, they would withdraw beneath the silvery canopy of the ancient trees; for it was there, according to St. Luke's account, that they often spent the night. Now one day, as they climbed the hill, the disciples began to ask, "Master, teach us to pray." And Jesus, standing in the midst of them, with the whole panorama of the Holy City stretching out behind Him like a symbol of the world, and at the very foot of the hill beyond the brook Cedron, the great mass of the temple buildings with their lofty towers, figures of the greatness of God, Jesus gave to them and to all mankind the sublime lesson: "When you pray, pray thus: 'Our Father, who art in Heaven . . .' "[77]

In modern times, at the spot that tradition points out as the place where the Lord's Prayer was composed, a devout princess was moved to construct a chapel with a kind of cloister; under its arches, porcelain tablets have been affixed to the walls upon which the Our Father is repeated in one archway after another in thirty-two languages. There the universe re-echoes

---

[75] Cf. Matt. 18:20.

[76] Matt. 17:1; Mark 9:1; Luke 9:28.

[77] Cf. Luke 11:1-2; Matt. 6:9.

in every voice and at every hour the ideal prayer which could have come only from Heaven.

Finally, most often no doubt, Jesus prayed alone. Let us consider this prayer more closely, first in its external conditions and then, as far as is possible to us, in its meaning.

∞

Aside from the temple and synagogue prayers, every Jew, in accordance with rabbinical prescriptions, was obliged to pray three times each day. It can hardly be doubted that in this, as in all respects, the Savior submitted to the laws of His people.

But it was especially in the evening that His prayer, free from all hindrance, was prolonged. Naturally, He must have allowed His body some rest, the indispensable rest; but it was short because it was free. The sleep of Jesus was not, like ours, a drowsiness rising from below as the magnetic pull of the earth whence we were drawn, which overcomes us with an irresistible force. It was a repose permitted, not stolen. His soul, master of itself, regulated the amount and the manner; and it postponed the hour so as to enjoy, before the material rest, its own perfect tranquillity.

Was it not right that after having spent the day in doing, preaching, working, suffering, and living His temporal life, which was a wretched one, after all, He should be able, when night fell and the earth gave itself to sleep, to enter completely, and not merely by the divine part of Himself, into the calm of eternity? During the day, He lived on earth; at eventide, He was lifted up again into Heaven.

And in order that this ascension of soul might have its symbol, Jesus loved to pray on the mountaintops. Often the

Gospels tell us, "He withdrew to the mountain alone. . . . He went up onto the mountain to pray."[78] The old prophets prayed in this wise. From time immemorial, the "high places,"[79] as the Bible calls them, had been considered the favored spot for the soul seeking divine intimacy. Jesus loved to pray thus.

At eventide, when heaven itself seems to retire, withdrawing its light unto itself, when the lofty triumph of the sun terminates in sober, silent emotion, Jesus parted from His friends. He climbed some lovely hillside. Leaving the earth and the day's cares far below, shaking off the dust of pedestrian roads on the grassy footpath, He went up into the realm of the stars. There, gradually invaded by peace from above, His soul expanded toward Heaven.

Like a ciborium wherein the consecrated bread rests, and which the priest lifts in his two hands to offer it to the sovereign Lord, so was the humanity of Jesus. He left aside, He forgot, if we may dare so to speak, the human, tangible, manifold, ephemeral aspect of His work, and entered into the ineffable. He broke into that colloquy with the Father which it is not given to man even to conceive — the unheard dialogue between God and God, the Infinite and the Immense, the Creator and Him who is more than a creature, between Him who is and the one who has become by grace Him who is. Who can tell us what transpired in the silent communication of that prayer? In the womb of night, which enlarges everything, of that night, which is so vast, which liberates objects from their exact limitations and transitory contours so as to wrap

---

[78] John 6:15; Mark 6:46; Luke 6:12 (Revised Standard Version).

[79] Cf. 3 Kings 3:3 (RSV = 1 Kings 3:3).

them in eternity, and which is consequently, as Dionysius the Areopagite[80] was accustomed to say, the most faithful image of God, Jesus, too, entered into the regions of immensity. This little world was no longer anything to Him. His soul soared into limitless space. There it radiated unto infinity, penetrating it with its twofold divine power — as God, principle of all things; as man, entrusted with all — bestowing life on all, impelling creatures into the mysterious paths whereby all things proceed; God and man, doing at once the work of God and the work of Christ, He performed and exacted, offered and received the great universal oblation.

And the dark planet revolved under His feet, unaware. And the stars pursued their nocturnal course, watching Him, like servants attending upon their master. They exhibited their stately glory before that point in space where their Creator tarried so far into the night.

Let us penetrate more deeply into the prayer of the Master — or at least try to. We cannot pretend to reach profounder depths; one would have to be of those who have experienced divine ecstasies. St. Paul, the man of the third Heaven,[81] and St. John, the eagle with the piercing, gentle eye,[82] those giants who, without physically leaving the earth,

---

[80] Dionysius the Areopagite, early Christian converted by St. Paul (Acts 17:34).

[81] Cf. 2 Cor. 12:2.

[82] The four living creatures mentioned in Revelation 4:7 have traditionally been regarded as symbols of the four Evangelists, the eagle representing St. John.

lived instantaneously in Heaven, like those mountains whose roots plunge deeply into the valley crevasses, while their summit gazes far off above the crest of the hills: these might tell us something about the prayer of Jesus. But they have taken the trouble to warn us that man is not permitted to speak of those hidden mysteries of Heaven.[83]

And yet they must be spoken of; let us try to analyze as well as we can the prayer of the Master. To what do His sentiments correspond? What outbursts of the soul do they excite?

Undoubtedly, the first is adoration. Adoration is the first expression of justice to which God lays claim.

God is. His very name substantiates His rights; for He is *Being*. His existence is absolute, unlimited, immutable, and necessary. Like a thousand rays from a focal point, being spreads from Him in all its forms. Intelligence, will, love, goodness, fruitfulness, justice, power — prolong this list unto infinity and each in its fullness, and all of it in unity, in perfect simplicity, and all eternally: that is God.

Moreover all other beings possessed of a reflection of these things, possess them only through Him, only in Him, without any possibility of depriving Him of their primordial possession; thus it is only justice for them to acknowledge before Him that they are nothing and that He alone is all. That is adoration. To adore is to recognize the whole of the object and the nothingness of the adorer. It is proclaiming that this object has every perfection, every right, all being. Adoration is nonentity swooning away and gladly expiring in the presence of Infinity. And that is what Jesus does.

---

[83] 2 Cor. 12:4.

He acknowledges that the creature is nothing, nothing but a breath from the divine mouth. He recognizes that He Himself is nothing from the standpoint of that humanity that He animates, marvelous as it is. "Why do you call me good?" He said one day to a young man who had addressed Him as "good Master." "Only one is good: God."[84] One alone is also great; and the human Christ, with all His glory, is but a ray broken loose from God. By adoration, then, He reascends humbly toward His source.

Enshrouded in the inebriating calm of an oriental night; under the scintillating stars, now faint, now burning like hearts afire; or else in the ghostly light of the moon, fringing her white robes with radiance, His humanity prostrated itself in expressible adoration. It drew to itself all creatures to make obeisance before the sovereign Lord. That wonderful art which nature is, its music, its painting, its sublime architecture: He made Himself their poet; in Him they sang the glory of God, and His heart beat the measure for the concert of creation. He Himself, a living universe epitomizing all creatures, offered Himself to Heaven as the representative of all things. And this was the world restored to the God who had brought it forth. His soul achieved for the first time this justice: God was adored as much as He deserves to be adored.

As a consequence of these rights that Jesus Christ recognized in His Father, sovereign rights implying sovereign dominion, He delivered into His hands His life, His personal life and the life of His work. The Father had His plan; His own duty was to follow it. There, in the stillness of night, He organized

---

[84] Cf. Mark 10:17-18.

His days. He regulated their every detail in intimate union with the Father. He encompassed with His glance the field of battle, the field of labor, and the field of death, which was to become the field of victory. And His heart followed His vision and accepted all in advance, obedient "even unto death."[85]

And the future? How did He look upon it? What did He say to God concerning it? How heavily did it weigh upon Him in His prayer? That is perhaps the greatest mystery in Christ. The thought is terrifying. The work of Christ on earth would, to all appearances, seem unworthy of Him.

He had come to uplift the world, to snatch it from the tyranny of evil and restore it to God. He said this, and the vigorous expressions He used gave sufficient evidence of the intensity of His desires: "I am come," He said, "to cast fire upon the earth, and what will I but that it be kindled."[86] But the earth was to be ice-cold toward Him. His immediate, personal labor — few Christians, no doubt, have realized this — was to meet with frustration.

His first ministry at Nazareth was a failure; they tried to hurl Him over a cliff.[87] His ministry in Galilee was repulsed; it ended with a curse. Finally, His death had no other explanation but defeat; and more than one has interpreted His last word from the cross — "It is finished"[88] — as the discouraged admission of one who bids farewell to every hope. This is a blasphemy, of course; but what is indeed true is that during His

---

[85] Phil. 2:8.

[86] Luke 12:49.

[87] Luke 4:29.

[88] John 19:30 (Revised Standard Version).

lifetime, Jesus managed only to sow the seed. He had declared, "The kingdom is like a grain of mustard seed, the smallest of all the seeds."[89] But He longed for a great tree, and the great tree would grow only in the course of centuries. How slowly! How laboriously! And in the course of what moving vicissitudes! Turn to the pages of history.

Some people imagine that the gospel spread like wildfire. That is false — absolutely false! The truth is that the seed produced its fruit "in patience,"[90] as the Savior declared.

Read St. Paul. Listen to his groanings. See him, exhausted with labors and trembling with fright. Consider those small churches that are formed, slowly, humbly, and then divided so as to form others.

And still later: look again. Certainly, there were some triumphs in the cause of God, miraculous triumphs — that is all we can call them. But the miraculous, in relation to the human elements cooperating with them: how meager it is in comparison with the desires of Christ!

The desires of Christ. What a furnace! That torrent of fire which could not be quenched by the sea's immensity: what did it find to devour that could in any way satiate its longing? How very little!

The ideal kingdom of God toward which He yearned with all the powers of His being will never exist. Never will the will of the Father be done "on earth as it is in Heaven,"[91] to use Christ's own words. And that immense prayer, that prayer of

---

[89] Cf. Matt. 13:31-32.
[90] Cf. Luke 21:19.
[91] Matt. 6:10.

flame, that prayer far-flung as space itself, which we call the Our Father, will never be for men more than a sublime utopia, an ideal toward which they tend but which they shall not achieve. And He, the Christ, must resign Himself to its non-achievement. All He can do is to fill up, by the gift of Himself, the void left by creatures; to supply for what they are not by what He is, what they cannot do by what He can, what they refuse by what He offers. That is one of His functions; and if He prolongs His prayer throughout the night, it is partly so that He may pour forth into the bosom of the Father the over-flow of His soul, which the human results of His labors did not satisfy.

Moreover, this substitution is intended to make up for the good that the future will refuse; it must also be exerted on be-half of that which it will accomplish, but after much procrasti-nation. Once more: it will take centuries, an accumulation of centuries, to build up the divine work. And on the debris of how many ruins! And over what heaps of rubbish!

Surely, God is a strange workman. He has methods that are disconcerting to our reason, but one thing is quite certain: He is not in a hurry. He carves the centuries out of infinity; what has He to do with economy?

See what He did for the earth. Through what terrifying series of transformations did He guide it, from nebula to life; from the first quiver of vitality in the depths of the sea up to man, who appears after thousands of centuries to gather in the heritage of the past, as the reaper arrives when the harvest is ripe.

Then, consider the history of humankind. What roads man has traveled! How slow his progress; from the pastoral, nomadic tribes to the great civilizations of the East, from these to the Roman Empire, from the Empire to our day, and from now into the unknown of history to be made. All of that is the work of God being accomplished and, therefore, the work of Christ; for all things have been placed in His hands, since it is His *Spirit* that must renew the face of the earth.[92]

But how slowly! How many stops, how many obstacles, how many setbacks! What a hopeless rate of progress! Even if God Himself is not in a hurry, wouldn't we expect Jesus as man to be anxious for the enhancement of the Father's honor? Can we not believe that He who saw the future from afar must have sighed ardently for it, summoned it forth by His yearnings, and been consumed with desire while He waited? And since He must indeed submit His will to the order established by the Father, must He not at least have offered His intense eagerness as a pledge of the reality to come?

∞

Such is the principal object of the interior prayer of Jesus. He adored, and He longed for God's glory. Did He not also desire on behalf of men? And as a result of this desire, did He not ask? I can hardly doubt that Jesus in His prayer thought of His own. One day, taking Simon Peter aside, He said to Him, "Simon, Simon, behold, Satan hath desired to have you, that he might sift you as wheat. But I have prayed for you, that your faith fail not."[93] No doubt, Simon was not the only one to benefit from the Master's prayer. He united all His own in His

[92] Ps. 103:30 (RSV = Ps. 104:30).
[93] Luke 22:31-32.

heart; all His own of the present and of the future and, consequently, all of us. It would be blasphemous to say that He did not foresee each of us, did not keep us in sight, did not expend in the service of each at least some throbbings of His heart.

And what did He ask for us? Everything, everything — without even forgetting the wretched problem of bread to eat, which none of us escapes, and other problems that are often urgent. He anticipated that and took pity on us; He said for us and with us, "Give us this day our daily bread."[94]

But it was especially with our soul that He was concerned. And what did He ask for on behalf of our soul? We shall understand it by considering what we are.

We are guilty, and we are weak. Because we are guilty, He begged pardon for us. Because we are weak, He begged — what? That temptation disappear? That evil withdraw from us and make no more assaults upon us? No. That is not what Jesus asked. He well knew that for each of us, as well as for the whole world, it is not good to be exempt from difficulties. It is in trial that the soul matures, not in inertia and slothfulness. If a general takes an interest in a soldier and holds him in some regard, does he send him to vegetate in the quartermaster or baggage department? He throws him into the thick of battle and desires only one thing for him: not repose but victory. That is the way with Jesus Christ.

Furthermore, does Jesus Christ always ask victory for His disciples? Ultimate victory, yes, for "He wills not the death of the sinner."[95] But immediate, complete victory such as would

[94] Luke 11:3.
[95] Cf. Ezek. 18:23; 2 Peter 3:9.

entail no failures, no. Obviously, He wishes it might be so; He tends toward it as a desirable objective; but to ask for it without qualification would be a departure from the conditions of our present life.

He is well aware that our best virtues are sometimes founded in our miseries. He who penetrates into the depths of souls, before whom alone the murky labyrinths come to light wherein our lives are entangled and lose their way: He knows by what path each soul can best travel. And sometimes this path is strewn with failures.

We would not dare to say so, had not great geniuses and great saints affirmed it before us; but they have done so, some of them after personal experience of its truth. Was it not St. Augustine,[96] a man whose authority cannot be impugned in such matters, who said these daring words: "To him who loves God all things turn to advantage, even his sins."[97]

There must be struggle, we have said; and there must also be defeat. Did not Jesus Christ leave His Apostles to taste it? The one He had called Cephas, "the rock,"[98] and to whom He had said, "Simon, Simon . . . I have prayed for you that your faith fail not," He permitted to fall three times, and under shameful circumstances.[99] Peter kept his faith, that is, his conviction regarding Jesus, his confidence, his attachment, his desire for the good, and that love which continues to flame in the depths of his soul at the moment of his falls; but he did fall,

---

[96] St. Augustine (354-430), Bishop of Hippo.
[97] Cf. Rom. 8:28.
[98] Matt. 16:18; John 1:42.
[99] Matt. 26:69-75.

and Jesus permitted it to be so. Why? Because He knew that in the realm of the supernatural, the first power of the soul is not strength, but humility; and humility is a pearl which can only be picked up out of the dust of defeat. We must realize how incurable we are before seeking the cure outside of ourselves.

Furthermore, Jesus was perfectly aware, when He let Simon Peter fall, that the future zeal of His apostle would be fed there as at its best source, and that this memory — bitter, never set at rest — would cause him to throw himself into labors, into martyrdom, just as the prick of the spur wounding its flanks urges the steed into the thick of the battle.

Let us turn to the scene after the Resurrection: "Simon Peter, lovest thou me?" "Lord, Thou knowest that I love Thee!" "Simon Peter, lovest thou me?" "Lord, Thou knowest that I love Thee." "Simon Peter, lovest thou me?"[100] A flood of tears poured from the eyes of the apostle. He understood. It was the triple denial the Master wished to recall to him. That thought — oh, how it penetrates into the quick of the soul, rendering it mad with grief! Yes, but it also touches those deep springs whose expansion will one day lift off mountains of suffering. And when the Savior concludes, after the threefold protestation of love that has effaced Peter's triple shame, when He says the words, "Feed my sheep,"[101] investing his repentance with all the faculties of pardoning others, Peter is already on the road to Rome, where the cross awaits him.

Let us recall the prayer of Christ in the midst of our temptations and anxieties. Let us join ours to it, which will

[100] John 21:15, 16, 17.
[101] John 21:17.

not increase its value, but will establish us in the dispositions necessary to profit by it for our soul's good.

For us, as well as for Christ, praying is ascending to the mountaintop, to the sources of strength and peace, of tranquillity and life. It is both fortifying ourselves and standing our guard, taking shelter under God's buckler and retempering our sword for the fight. It is acknowledging that we are nothing, but that we can do all things in Him.[102] When we have gone thus far, let us have no fear. The rest depends upon Heaven.

On the day when Jesus Christ, a victim of the carnal enthusiasm of the crowd who wished to proclaim Him king, found Himself obliged to withdraw from their indiscreet ovation, He went off as usual to the mountain. And while He prayed, He saw from afar His disciples down there on the lake, struggling against the waves. One of those sudden squalls typical of the Sea of Galilee, which become angry in less than a quarter of an hour, had imperiled the apostles' craft. Doubtless, they thought of Him in their distress. And He, powerful and kind, having finished His prayer, came straightaway. Because He had to go directly and any delay would have been fatal, He came walking on the waters.[103]

He does the same for His faithful. After having prayed, He will come; He will walk on the waters of adversity that form our life, or of that tempestuous sea, which is our soul. He will say, "It is I! Fear not!"[104] And, as in the Gospel account, the boat will reach the shore.

---

[102] Cf. Phil. 4:13.
[103] John 6:15-19.
[104] John 6:20.

The shore is peace of heart; it is safety, after trouble or defeat; it is the recommencement of life on a more solid foundation. Finally, the shore is Heaven. Heaven, the ultimate goal of our earthly efforts; the abode of permanent peace amid the joys of the reward; the eternal harbor toward which Christ impels our craft under the breath of His prayer, that place of peace where the just man will come to port.

Chapter Six

∞

His Enemies:
He Combats
Injustice

∞

In his letter to the Romans, St. Paul makes a statement that is frequently quoted and often meditated upon both by those who govern and by those who obey: "There is no power but from God."[105] Even the powers deriving from men, based upon a freely accepted contract, or in fact upon force, come from God. For after all, no man has the right to govern another. We are free, and whatever superiority nature or opportunity may have bestowed upon anyone in particular does not confer the right to hold another person in subjection. What, then, enables one man or group of men to exercise command? It can only be a sort of delegation whose first principle is God Himself.

God has made man a social being, and since the social group cannot survive without a bond, that is to say, without authority, this authority operates in the name of God, and it is toward God that the homage we render it returns. This being true, Jesus could not dispense Himself from honoring that authority and, in the measure allowed by His mission, submitting to it. Not that He owed obedience to anyone; but He owed everyone an example. It is hardly necessary to say that in this regard as in every other He gave that example.

[105] Rom. 13:1.

As a private individual, if we may dare to use the expression, He obeyed the laws of His people in all respects. He willed to submit to circumcision;[106] He observed the Sabbath;[107] He paid the tribute;[108] He attended the synagogue and went to Jerusalem for the great feasts.[109] In His public action, it would seem that we should find Him still more respectful by reason of the more serious consequences that would result from His conduct. In His time, especially, there was cause for working, through a respect for institutions and the men who represented them, toward the pacification of souls.

The Jewish nation was profoundly upset. Incapable of enduring patiently the yoke of Rome, which seemed to them a profanation, they rose up periodically in outbursts of nationalism that developed into rage. Frequent riots took place; they were suppressed by means of bloodshed. But, as always happens, this blood, drenching the roots of hatred, caused them to spring up with more vitality than ever. Two thousand rebels had been crucified after one of these revolts, at the very gates of the city. It was an appalling sight, which caused roars of fury from those self-styled patriots who were known as Zealots. The effect, by way of pacification, in these fierce hearts, was a kind of terrifying enthusiasm. Beyond all this, there were the usual internal dissensions: rivalries between sects, struggles for power, smoldering jealousy, clamorous disputes, suspicions, rancor, denouncements, and civil war between souls.

---

[106] Luke 2:21.

[107] Luke 4:16.

[108] Matt. 17:23-26 (RSV = Matt. 17:24-27).

[109] Luke 2:41-42; John 7:10.

He Combats Injustice

If Jesus loved His native land, it would seem that He should have acted in such a way as to heal the rifts, so that, by rallying all forces behind the legitimate authority, the nation might be once more in a position to defend the common good. In periods of turmoil and dissension, when all the elements of a people disunite and drop away, leaving it, like a corpse, to the ravages of corruption, the duty of patriots becomes clearly outlined. However discredited the government may be, they must join forces around it, not strive against it under the pretext of political opposition or personal preferences. The commonweal is in danger; the only remedy is to be found in united action; and even if this action might be less than ideal, they must submit and obey.

Jesus loved His country. He was no stranger to that sentiment, half-instinctive, half-deliberate, which is known as patriotism; rather, in Him it was more elevated and perfect than in us. Instead of that feeling of weakness that, in us, identifies patriotism, however sacred, with our inherent weakness, so as to incline us to look upon the homeland, our birthplace, our native soil, as a kind of refuge — such as the safe harbor is to the fisherman during a storm, or a mother's arms to her timid, frail child — in Jesus, all was magnanimous and perfect. He loved His people, and although His conceptions infinitely surpassed our ideas of a fatherland, they nevertheless encompassed them, as the infinite includes the atom. As man, He always cherished a special preference for that soil from which His Father had caused Him to spring.

Notwithstanding all this, when we read the Gospel, we find Jesus constantly at odds with the authorities. His activity in Jerusalem especially, when He periodically returned there to celebrate the festivals, was a perpetual conflict with those in power. Why was this?

The fact is that, however respectful He might have been toward authority, and however desirous He always was of keeping the peace, Jesus could not abdicate or, still less, forget His mission.

Respect is not a force; it is a limit. It avoids destruction, but effects no construction. Now, Jesus had come to construct and to set a force in motion. If, therefore, He encountered resistance on His way, there was only one thing for Him to do: break it down. In every collision, He must safeguard His liberty for the benefit of His mission.

This must be understood in approaching a study of the relations of Jesus with the Jewish authorities. There is a false liberty that consists in judging without any right, reproving without mandate, condemning without jurisdiction; but there is no reason to fear anything of the sort on the part of Him who possesses all rights and in whom all wisdom abides. His conduct will always be prudent. Nevertheless, He will always succeed in making it evident that He is the Master, master of His deeds and master of Himself.

There is an episode that manifests this attitude in action; it is reported to us by St. Luke. Jesus was in Galilee and, consequently, under the jurisdiction of Herod. As He was preaching before a great crowd of people, some Pharisees approached Him and, feigning concern for His safety, said to Him, "Depart from here, for Herod intends to kill Thee." Jesus replied, "Go, and tell that fox: Behold, I cast out demons and I heal the sick today and tomorrow; and the third day I shall have finished. But I must walk today, tomorrow, and the following day. For it is not fitting that a prophet should perish outside of Jerusalem."[110]

What a declaration! What serene majesty! What simplicity! What mastery! Isn't He really free? Doesn't He show Himself truly in control?

"Go, and tell that fox": He has the right name for that crowned blackguard, that cowardly cutthroat. Will He inspire courage in those who, in times of faint-heartedness and decay, having the right and the duty of speaking, think they serve God by retreating into a craven silence? Will He give a lesson in the prerogatives of truth to those who, in the same eras, dare to close the mouths of Christ's representatives under pretext of prudence and charity? As if one could not be prudent without being pusillanimous! As if one served the truth only by keeping it under a bushel basket! And as if one loved one's brethren only to the extent that one abandoned them to the trickery and violence of their enemies!

And what were they to say to that fox of a Herod? Tell him: See, I am casting out devils; I am making the sick well; I am accomplishing my work today, tomorrow, and the next day. After that, it will be the hour of the powers of darkness. I shall manage to suffer what must be suffered; meanwhile, I am doing what I must do. After these three days, there will be death; but death because I will it, and death where I will it; and where I will it is not in your domain, King of Galilee, but in Jerusalem.

"It is not fitting that a prophet should perish outside of Jerusalem." A soldier must die in the breach, a laborer at his work, a pastor in the midst of his people; a prophet must die in

---

[110] Cf. Luke 13:31-33.

Jerusalem. But in the meantime, I go on my way. Today, tomorrow, and the day after belong to me. I accomplish my work in spite of you; I shall do it, if necessary, by resisting you. I am not afraid, and I will not allow you to put me in irons.

Such is Jesus' attitude in the face of authority. No provocation, but always and regardless of circumstances: liberty. As a matter of fact, Jesus would not often be in a position to use this liberty in regard to Herod. Only later would Jesus meet him, and then only in passing.[111] It was otherwise with the Jewish powers.

Jesus established Himself on a religious plane; but in Jerusalem, religion and politics had but one concern; church and state were mutually involved. Hence, the Sanhedrin, the high priests, and the Pharisees and scribes could not but intervene, by force of circumstances. In which direction would they do so? That was the vital question. As for Jesus, He would make no modification whatsoever in His work. As for them, they could accept Him, understand Him, and even cooperate with Him. But would they?

We are well aware of the answer. However, it might be worthwhile to analyze the motives; more than one lesson is hidden behind this strange drama of Jesus' relations with the powers that be.

∞

In the milieu of which we are speaking, Jesus had two forces against Him that never forgive an attack on them. The past was against Him, and passion was against Him.

[111] Cf. Luke 23:8-11.

The past is indeed a power. It is the root whence we have sprung, and the more deeply that root is buried in the earth, the more stubbornly it resists. We have an instinct for the eternal, the permanent: it is a sign of our destiny. But it easily becomes a formidable aberration and danger, because it is difficult to detach oneself sufficiently from what is always more or less selfish in this sentiment.

The past is what has made us; it is ourselves, in a sense, that we are defending in it. That is why the struggle on behalf of the past takes on, in some narrow minds, the fierceness and blindness of the battle for life. This can be avoided but only with difficulty, because then one must go out of oneself, disengage, detach, raise oneself somehow beyond time; and as a line of conduct, it is not within the scope of everybody.

Scarcely anyone can succeed in this completely except a genius, unless it be a saint. But genius, like sanctity, is a rare article. Like the high wave that rises above the tide and towers beyond the white-crested billows, so in the ocean of humanity, occasionally one head is lifted up and considers the scene: that is genius.

But it does not take long to count such personalities. What is commonplace is being in a groove and desperately anxious to remain in it. What is commonplace is for the established powers, the constituted institutions, to seek to maintain themselves without bothering about anything else. Self-interest absorbs them; new ideas upset them; daring frightens them. They prefer to consider the past rather than the future; and since any forward step has to be taken by walking over what is falling into ruin and upon the debris of what can no longer survive, it is not at all surprising that the representatives of former times should rebel against any initiative and strongly oppose movements of renewal.

Now, Jesus was an innovator to a degree that few suspect. He finds Himself face-to-face with Judaism, a religion inspired by God but in the capacity of precursor, and therefore with an incomplete status that had no further reason for existence once the Christ had come. He came therefore, this Christ, with the fire of His word, to consume the dry wood, which was henceforth useless. Did that not suffice to render Him suspect even to the relative good faith that He must have encountered at the start?

Nowadays we no longer recognize to what a degree the doctrine of Jesus was subversive. Imbued as we are with Christian principles, which have governed human thought for centuries, we have no idea how strangely new they were in the eyes of a Jew in the age of Tiberius.[112]

No doubt Jesus presented His credentials; hence we cannot exonerate those whom He condemned. But in what terms did He refer to them? "If I had not done among them the works that no one else did," He says, "they would not have sin, but now they have seen and have hated both me and my Father."[113] Obviously, the crime of the Jews was not that they found Jesus' doctrine strange and almost scandalous; it was that they had refused to verify His claims and had persisted in looking upon Him merely as a revolutionary without warrant.

It is nonetheless true that there was a pretext for opposition and that such opposition had a good chance of succeeding. No

---

[112] Tiberius (42 B.C.-A.D. 37), Roman emperor from 14-37.
[113] John 15:24 (Revised Standard Version).

one is unaware of the terms in which Jesus expressed His law: "Moses told you *that*; but I tell you *this*. Moses commanded *that*; as for me, I order you to do *this*."[114] Is it conceivable to speak thus to Jews? To stand up in the face of Moses and reform his law? It was at once sacrilege and a crime of high treason against the nation, for in the eyes of a Jew, Moses was the race, the religion, and the state. No one could touch Moses without pulling down the whole edifice.

Jesus announced the destruction of the temple;[115] but the temple, too, was the race, religion, and state. He attacked the clergy of the day; and the clergy was also race, religion, and state. He spoke to Gentiles; He predicted their incorporation into His Church.[116] Now, Jewish exclusivism was fifteen centuries old; it had been inaugurated by God Himself; and if it had outlived its time, if the hour had come when, in religious thinking, there would no longer be either Jew or pagan, Greek or barbarian,[117] but just humanity, it must be acknowledged that here was a teaching singularly difficult to inject into those mentalities.

What if hypocrisy and vice made common cause with narrowness and intolerance? That is just what happened among the influential in Jerusalem.

Some have wondered how it came about that Jesus, who was "meekness itself," could have shown Himself so severe toward the doctors and high priests. Stated thus, the question bears

[114] Cf. Matt. 5:21-22, 27-28, 33-34, 38-39, 43-44.
[115] Matt. 24:1-2; Mark 13:1-2; Luke 21:5-6.
[116] Cf. Matt. 8:11; Luke 13:29.
[117] Cf. Rom. 10:12.

the marks of a very common delusion. It consists in looking upon Jesus only as the "Lamb of God,"[118] the "meek and humble"[119] individual, the man of pleasant parables and gentle speech, if not as the youth portrayed in pious art with curling locks, a delicate beard, and the hands of a woman. Jesus Christ is not exactly that. Meek and humble of heart He is indeed; above all, He is so; but when it becomes necessary, He is terrifying! He presents to us all the aspects of God. Two things have been affirmed about God: He is the Father, in whose sight every hair of our head has been counted,[120] and He is the one who has said of Himself, "It is a fearful thing to fall into the hands of the living God!"[121] The more His mercy is assured to the repentant and His pity to the weak, the more adamant He is toward the proud and the perfidious.

Let us consider what sort of men were in power during Jesus' public life. We shall then understand His strictures.

A distinction must be made between two aristocracies, both of which Jesus was obliged to combat: the priestly aristocracy and the intellectual aristocracy. The former, composed largely of Sadducees, comprised the high priest, the elders, the pontificating priests, and the scribes. They composed what was known as the Sanhedrin, an assembly that was at once a tribunal, a parliament, and a council. These self-styled Sadducees,

[118] John 1:29.
[119] Matt. 11:29.
[120] Matt. 10:30; Luke 12:7.
[121] Cf. Heb. 10:31.

that is to say, *just* men, were often avaricious and cunning. Many of them trafficked in piety and had little regard for it. It is the right of the priest, St. Paul says, to live by the altar; but woe to the priest who lives by the altar and does not labor for it.[122] These men were satisfied with the easy externals of an official piety. A detestable combination of pride and baseness, brutality and cleverness, tyranny and servility, they ground down the people, crushed them with their haughtiness and ostentation, and then turned around to grovel before the henchmen of Rome.

They were conservatives; that goes without saying. But only God knows what this intrinsically honorable title sometimes conceals within itself of fierce egotism and meanness. He is estimable who is conservative about what he believes to be good and true; but he is detestable and justly despised who is conservative in all things, conservative of his own ease, comfort, and social standing. No one has a right to set his prejudices in the way of advancing truth, his selfish interests before the development of the commonweal, or his stupid conventionality athwart God's designs for human progress. It is a crime against God and man; it is the sin against the Holy Spirit, the "unforgivable sin."[123]

At the time of Jesus, many of the Jewish high priests were conservative after this fashion. They did not take Moses too seriously themselves; but for them Moses spelled power, honor, and profit, and so they were always quoting him. They were the champions of the established order, the guardians of the

[122] Cf. 1 Cor. 9:14, 16.
[123] Cf. Matt. 12:31, 32; Luke 12:10.

status quo. To be on good terms with the Romans, to maintain their influence over the people, to be well-off, and to live off the fat of the land: that was their only desire. To them, religion was not an end, but a means; Moses was not their master, but their provider. As for the Messiah, either they did not give him a thought or they considered him in purely abstract terms that did not bother them; or else, if they condescended to expect him, they felt pretty sure of making him their tool and thereby enhancing their own glory and profit.

Such were many of the priestly party at the time of Jesus.

Besides this clerical aristocracy, there was the intellectual elite: doctors, scribes, almost all of them Pharisees, that is to say, *set apart, distinguished,* men of one book, namely, God's book, but writing the commentaries of men, and often, the commentaries of narrow, stubborn men, inflated with pride, who look down upon those who have not attained to the "true knowledge," as they call it, and understand nothing about the *ways of God.*

In their opinion, salvation consists in a multitude of observances that they catalog like the prescriptions of an apothecary. Morality becomes casuistry, religion a technique. If you are ignorant of the prescription, you are lost.

Assuredly, even among the Pharisees were some whose motive was love, for they were to come forth, on the morrow of Jesus' death, as eminent Christians: for instance, St. Paul, who was a convinced Pharisee, just as out of the Sanhedrin would come Joseph of Arimathea and Nicodemus.[124] But these were only exceptions.

[124] Acts 23:6; Mark 15:43; John 3:1-2.

Too many of the Pharisees had a high opinion of their own worth. Clerical functionaries or professional savants, they often displayed the same arrogance, the same contempt for the lowly; they concealed the same avarice and the same immorality. Many of them were haughty men, living on other people's virtue and betraying virtue in their own hearts; wily casuists who imposed upon consciences insupportable burdens that they were careful not to touch with their fingertips; "whited sepulchers,"[125] as the Master called them; plastered faces, hateful to look upon; men at once smooth-tongued and vicious: how well He knew them!

In Solomon's Porch, He said to them, pointing out below the Mount of Olives opposite them the freshly carved tombstones that even today stand out in the Valley of Cedron, "Do you see those sepulchers? They are like you! They are whitewashed on the outside, but within they are filled with bones and corruption. You did well in adorning them; they are your concern. Your fathers killed the prophets who sleep there; you are finishing their work. That is right; you are indeed their sons!"[126]

Under such conditions, what kind of relations could there have been between Jesus and the princes of the people?

Just consider how He irked them. They couldn't lie any more. They could no longer deceive the crowd. That clear glance of Jesus saw right through their sophistries. That manifest truth that shone forth in all His words immediately drew to His cause those whom they had tried so hard to win over.

[125] Matt. 23:4, 27.
[126] Cf. Matt. 23:27, 29, 31-32.

Then, all the sharp practices, unjust profits, and acts of cruelty and indecency that took refuge behind the walls of the temple, sprinkled with lustral water to give a semblance of purity — all of that was dragged out into the open and there overwhelmed with scorn. It was too much. They had to defend themselves at any cost and to silence, before it became all-powerful, this murmur that was rising imperiously in the steps of the new prophet.

This explains their frame of mind.

Spurred on by the terror that gripped them and the envy gnawing at them, we see them taking the field. They will seek out false witnesses;[127] they will send agents to try to trip Him up in His speech;[128] they will beleaguer Him with malicious equivocation and tricky questions;[129] they will mingle with the crowds to spread hateful lies: "He is a winebibber and a glutton. He associates with sinners. He is the enemy of our people. He practices witchcraft and trafficks with the demons. . . ."[130] It is a warfare of foul play, allied to chicanery and underhandedness.

What can Jesus be expected to do in the face of such opposition — avoid an encounter? He cannot. It would mean surrendering the field, renouncing His mission, stopping the mouth of truth. Is that possible? Would such mollifying be acceptable at a price like that?

Mildness does not consist in hating nothing; still less does it consist in declaring oneself on the side of evil before attempting

[127] Matt. 26:60.
[128] Luke 11:53-54.
[129] Matt. 22:15.
[130] Cf. Matt. 9:34; Mark 2:16; Matt. 11:19.

to remedy it. That would be spinelessness, an utter lack of character. This is detestable because it attributes equal value to good and evil; because, instead of that vigorous condemnation that even poets extol, it presents only a pleasant grimace, regardless of whom it faces. Such an attitude is cowardly. One must hate evil with the same intensity as one loves the good.

Jesus indeed loved the good. With all the vehemence of a human soul and with the infinity of a divine nature, He loved it. What would you expect of Him, then? With what eye could He look upon these hypocrites, these men of lucre and filth, these traitors? How would He handle their intrigues, calculated to effect nothing less than the stifling of His work and, as He said, closing the door of the kingdom of Heaven, by which they themselves would not enter?[131] There was only one thing He could do: unmask them and, on the day when the occasion presented itself, put His foot into that nest of vipers[132] at the risk of meeting His death there.

This explains the violent denunciations of which the Gospel gives an account. Some people are scandalized by them. But it would be scandalous not to find them there; concern for His mission and that indescribable desire for the salvation of men that burned within Him had of necessity to produce in Jesus these outbursts of passion against the obstacle and those who were responsible for it. While He has compassion for those who commit sin out of weakness, He can produce only indignation against those who defend, cultivate, organize, and exploit sin. He pursues these with His hatred, the hatred born

[131] Cf. Matt. 23:13.
[132] Cf. Matt. 12:33.

of that love which makes the mother hen the enemy of the hawk and the lioness a fury protecting her cubs.

Yes, it is love for His children that throws Him into a towering rage against those who would snatch them away from Him. His soul was a burning furnace whence issued a devouring flame; but its fires were kindled only at the hearth of charity. Nevertheless, His words could be veritable thunderbolts, anathemas that shook the earth. On certain occasions, He gave Himself up to actions that seemed like madness. He drove before Him, with a whip of cords, those who carried on business in the temple.[133] He crushed the Pharisees, denouncing them before God and men, threatening them with unspeakable retribution.[134] And this was the cry of that love "strong as death," of that jealousy "hard as Hell," spoken of in the Canticle.[135] And it would conclude with a flood of tears: "Jerusalem, Jerusalem! Thou who killest the prophets sent by God, how many times would I not have gathered together thy children, as the hen gathers her chicks under her wings; but thou wouldst not!"[136]

Does Jesus Christ not gain in stature by all the indignation He thus manifests in behalf of truth and justice? His example has been followed. And this is the explanation of many a crisis in the history of Christian civilizations. Even in the Church, the spirit behind the sins of the Pharisees who opposed Jesus is not always dead. Neither is Jesus Christ dead: He survives in

[133] John 2:15.

[134] Cf. Matt. 23:35-36; Luke 11:50-51.

[135] Cant. 8:6 (RSV = Song of Sol. 8:6).

[136] Luke 13:34.

His Church. And the clash is always ready to be produced, and the motives are invariably the same.

Power is not a school of virtue. When it does not encounter perverse men, it more often than not assumes the charge of perverting them. And since the Church is not perfect either, but mingles a human and therefore fallible element with the Christ whom She represents, the struggle is not nearing its end; no doubt it will fill the ages to come.

What attitude should we have toward this conflict? One that is unprejudiced, first of all, and then one imbued with the desire to do our part on the side of good.

We must allow to each power its domain; we must deplore the encroachments that may have occurred at certain epochs on the part of men who represented the Church. Such things have happened; it would be of no avail to deny them, and besides, it would indicate a lack of honesty. Let the truth prevail even when it hurts.

But let us be convinced that this is not the essence of the debate between the Church and the powers of this world. These are human vicissitudes such as no institution can avoid, and which are only too well explained by the intoxication and delusions of power. The substance of the matter is elsewhere; it is the same as it was at the time of Christ.

To the pride and injustice of the high priests, Christ was an embarrassment. The Church, too, is embarrassing, with Her dignity and the superb independence She displays. She is incapable of bending the knee except before God — but before men? Never. She is outspoken, come what may; and even amid the universal degeneracy of character, She preserves Her high-souled, honorable attitude toward duty.

Of course that becomes irritating. It exasperates people; for it does not permit them to enjoy peacefully their ill-gotten success; it disturbs certain schemes that seemed to be very advantageous, since these importunate protests open the eyes of well-intentioned people after great pains had been taken to win them over. Then what happens? These unjust powers foment plans against the Church, as they once did against Christ.

We shall not be able to change this. It is the normal state of affairs here on earth. The truth is like those knights errant who slept under their armor and only seemed to be leaning on their spear. Our problem is to stand for the right, that is, for the Master, and to cooperate insofar as we are able in the triumph of the good.

Chapter Seven

His Chosen Ones:
He Reveals the
Depths of Love

∾

One word seems to sum up better than all others the relationship of Jesus with His disciples: *kindness.* Men interpret this
word in a restricted, often an innocuous sense; but here it lays
hold of its fullness and even a higher significance.

Kindness lavishing its gifts, kindness yielding to another,
kindness supporting, forgiving, and crowning all with the sur-
render of self: all of this is to be found in the dealings of Jesus
with His own.

Jesus' calling of His disciples is the first manifestation of
this kindness and the first act in His relationship with them.
We know under what conditions it takes place: it is as if by
chance that Jesus collects His coworkers along the way.

On the banks of the Jordan, after John the Baptist had borne
witness, two of his listeners, Galilean fishermen who had come
there on pilgrimage, approach Jesus. "What do you seek?" He
asks them. "Master, where livest Thou?" "Come and see."
They go, and they abide with Him. The next day, they seek
out their brothers Simon and James: "We have found the Messiah!" And their brothers follow them, speak with Jesus, and
are won over.[137] A fifth crosses His path just as He is preparing

[137] John 1:38-41.

to leave. "Follow me," Jesus tells him; and he follows Jesus.[138] A little further on, as He is re-entering Galilee, He encounters Nathanael, seated under a fig tree in Cana; and He commandeers him.[139] Arriving in Capernaum, He walks by the customs office, sees Matthew the tax collector, and calls him.[140] And so it is with the rest.

There is no need to remark that all these chance meetings are arranged with far-seeing purpose by a sovereign will. The true name of chance is God; especially in all that concerns the redemptive work, everything is intended, arranged, and adapted with divine artistry. Furthermore, in order to make this quite evident, from His very first encounter, He bestows on some of His disciples names characteristic of their mission.[141] This is prophesying; the introduction of prophecy into vocations so simple that they might have seemed chance invitations gives them a touch of eternity.

A little later, when He decides definitely to form the apostolic group, indicating to each his position and function, He spends a whole night in prayer on the mountain. Not until morning, coming down to the shore of the lake, does He proceed to select the foundations of His Church: an evident mark of the depth of His deliberations.

And yet, they were certainly nothing worth boasting about, these disciples. Except for one of them who seemed to have some education they were all poor folk without influence or

---

[138] John 1:43.
[139] Cf. John 1:48.
[140] Matt. 9:9.
[141] Cf. Matt. 16:18; Mark 3:17.

culture. They were nobodies; from the Master alone they were to receive all; and how well off He was who had adopted them! From the very first day, He made them rich by revealing the future to them.

The future: how did it present itself before the excited gaze of the Apostles? What image of the future did they form for themselves?

Here, it would be dangerous to risk a reply; nevertheless it seems evident that they did not have a very clear idea of their prospective mission. They were initiated little by little; only step by step did they enter upon their career. No matter: were not all the treasures of the morrow implicit in the obscure summons of today, just as each plant is already contained potentially in its seed? And do we not have reason to believe that, if they had known how far their ambitions might extend, these weak men would have been bewildered by the disproportion between their persons and that preordination?

To be the foundations of the Church; to cooperate to an admirable extent in what constitutes the whole of the universe, since it is nothing less than salvation; to lead the advance of the nations that would pass along through the centuries without stopping until they reached the threshold of eternity: such was their destiny. They were not aware of it; but they did know one thing that even then must have filled them with gratitude. They knew that they were to "bear fruit";[142] that was the image the Master liked to use.

Is there any more magnanimous gift in the world than such fecundity?

[142] Cf. John 15:16.

If the Creator, St. Thomas Aquinas[143] tells us, had given us only our being, He would have reserved to Himself that which is best. But He treated His creatures with greater beneficence. He gave them being and the power to communicate being, life and the giving of life, action and becoming the source of action. That is why fruitfulness of life in every domain has something divine about it. That is why anyone who rejects it is mad as well as guilty. That is why the profaners of those sacred bonds that unite soul and body, those who dare to make of God's workshop, of that nursery of eternity known as Christian marriage, an egotistical, shameful commerce, provoke the wrath of Heaven and deserve the contempt of men. That is why, furthermore, the man who could manage, with brain or brawn, to be useful to his fellowman, to produce a beneficial effect upon a family, a community, or a nation, and yet withdraws into slothful inertia, is a despicable coward. Finally, that is why one whom God calls, like the disciples, to spiritual fecundity, to the communication and development of divine gifts, will never have voice enough to bless the Master, heart enough to enjoy the favor, or energy enough to make himself worthy of it.

Jesus owed it to His chosen ones to teach them to appreciate that truth. "It is not you who have chosen me," He said to them. "It is I who have chosen you."[144] Don't think that in coming to me, you deserve the credit and are doing me a favor; in this bargain, it is you who receive and I who give; you have

---

[143] St. Thomas Aquinas (c. 1225-1274), Dominican philosopher and theologian.

[144] John 15:16.

offered yourselves to me, and by becoming mine, you become greater. You are the channel carrying the life that I am bringing. By diffusing yourselves throughout the world, which you shall divide among you presently, you shall be like rivers transporting life across the plains; like clouds that float, pregnant with fertility. You are the main branches of the great tree of which I myself am the trunk; and as the divine sap rises and spreads unceasingly, the faith of the world will cling to you as the rich foliage to the arms of a mighty oak.

This was the meaning of the very simple invitation addressed to the disciples. It was to be expected that this gift, the initial favor preceded by no merit on their part, would be followed nevertheless by all the consequences it implied.

The first of these consequences was intimacy.

∞

At the outset, one cannot help finding something strange, almost shocking, in this intimacy of the Master with His disciples. Jesus Christ is everyone's man: it would seem that He should not belong in a particular way to anyone. By remaining solitary in His own life, He would control from above the mission to be accomplished.

Jesus Christ is God: from that aspect, intimacy seems not only unbecoming, but even absurd. What intimacy can there be between God and men?

Intimacy means equality — equality arrived at, if not inherent. It is a mingling of lives; it is a brotherhood of hearts; it is an accepted openness between them; it is the leveling of one soul with another; it is a communion of thoughts, desires, interests, and loves, with a mutual, entire freedom to penetrate and to judge one another always and to the very depths. Hence, what intimacy could there be between Jesus Christ and men? Men are so small, so weak, so obtuse, and so empty. And He is so preeminent, so far beyond this world, beyond this life. Is it not the destiny of the great to live alone, not to permit just anyone to penetrate into that inner recess of the soul, which is called intimacy? More than one genius has had friends; but this is true only of a facile genius. The transcendent kind, the human gods, the awe-inspiring, such as Michelangelo, Shakespeare, Beethoven, Dante, and even above and beyond these, the men set apart as sacred, such as Isaiah or Moses: these had no friends. They had confidants; they had protégées, satellites of their glory, assistants in their work, servants whose hearts were passionately devoted to them; but not intimates in the true sense of the word. Their souls were too lofty; their atmosphere was too rare for the respiration of mere humans. They were, so to speak, marked with a sign, terrifying and holy.

How much greater than all of them was the Divine Master! No human soul can be compared to His; no mind can pretend to rival or even remotely imitate His mind. Who could flatter himself with even being His inferior, without becoming insulting and absurd? To be inferior is still drawing a comparison, and with Him no comparison is possible. His level? Infinity. His span? Immensity. His concerns? Those of God Himself. Who, then, can become His intimate? Who can live in that atmosphere and gaze upon those horizons without flinching? No one!

All of this is true; but something else is involved here in addition to greatness. There is the divine condescension that creates, beside the infinite Jesus, a Jesus reduced, as it were, to our size, a Jesus "who lets Himself be handled" — as a great man has said — who can be immense, beyond all immensity, without making us feel how small we are. This is how He manifests Himself in the Gospel.

Tradition asserts that the Savior tempered the brilliance of His eyes because their great power was ill-adapted to the daily encounters of life. What is certainly true is that He tempered the brilliance of His soul and that He was capable, when he so pleased, of appearing on a level with other souls as a divinely attractive friend. That is how He dealt with His disciples. He put Himself on their level; He presented a basis for fellowship, for intimate confidences, for familiar dialogue, for loyal affection, and for a certain discreet playfulness that we barely glimpse in the Gospels.

When the Divine Master is about to multiply the loaves, on the slopes overlooking the lake, He sees Philip beside Him; knowing his simplicity, of which he was to give more than one proof, He says to him, doubtless in a gently teasing way, "Philip, where shall we find bread enough to feed everyone?" He asked this to see what he would say, comments the Evangelist. And Philip is taken in: "Two hundred pennyworth of bread would not suffice," he exclaims, "so that each may have a little!"[145] This familiar pleasantry indicates the good humor that prevailed in the relationship of Jesus with His disciples.

Notice the fine distinction in such matters. It is not laughter: a laugh is heavy, akin to the material; often it involves an element of pride and malevolence; at any rate, it suggests a

[145] Cf. John 6:5-7.

lack of self-possession, since it usually escapes from us without the control of the will. Here it is a smile, kindly, noble, moderate, identified with the spirit, just as everything should be in a superior nature such as that of the Master.

Ordinarily, the tone Jesus assumed with His followers was one of gentle gravity, full of simplicity and dignity. He calls them His "friends,"[146] His "children,"[147] His "little children,"[148] and His "little flock."[149] He explains to them in private what He has taught the crowd. "To you," He says, "it is given to understand the mysteries of the kingdom of Heaven, of which I speak to the rest in parables."[150] He often takes them aside to converse with them alone. On the roads between towns, He instructs and consoles them. He takes care of them like a watchful mother, inviting them to rest when the journey has been long, blessing their sleep while He Himself goes off to pray.

Again, at midday, when the heat becomes unbearable and the eastern sun, frightful and sometimes even death-dealing, sheds its blinding rays upon the path, He leads them apart, under some great tree or into one of those caves that can be found in great numbers under the rocky hills of Judea, and there, forming a circle about Him, they listen to His words. And His message pours forth, His teachings accumulate, His confidences are prolonged, the hours pass by, delightful and

[146] John 15:15.
[147] John 21:5.
[148] John 13:33.
[149] Luke 12:32.
[150] Cf. Luke 8:10.

profitable, while they await the hard labors to come; and the disciples feel themselves gradually penetrated by that love to which He sets no limits other than those of the heavenly Father. "As my Father has loved me," He says, "so do I love you."[151] "Whosoever hears you, hears me; he who despises you, despises me; he who receives you, receives me."[152] "I solemnly assure you, Sodom and Gomorrah will be treated less rigorously than the town which rejects you."[153]

Sometimes His overflowing heart bursts forth in effusions of tenderness, not that soft tenderness that is the prevalence of sense over intellect, but the generous affection recognized by truly great hearts.

One day He was speaking to a crowd in the presence of some Pharisees; His speech was forceful, and the disciples, as usual, had formed a circle about Him. Now, it happened that in the midst of His discourse, "His mother and His brethren arrived," declares the Evangelist. And when someone announced it to Him, saying, "Thy mother and Thy brethren are here, asking for Thee," He, all absorbed in what He had been speaking about, His soul a prey to intense emotion, exclaimed, "Who is my mother, and who are my brethren?" Then stretching forth His hand toward His disciples and looking at them tenderly, one by one, He said, "Here are my mother and my brethren! For whosoever does the will of my Father who is in Heaven is my brother and my sister and my mother."[154] Here

[151] Cf. John 15:9.
[152] Cf. Luke 10:16.
[153] Cf. Matt. 10:15.
[154] Mark 3:31-35.

we encounter a sublimely graded development of affection, ascending from a union based on force of circumstances to another based on sheer delight, mingling them together in that abyss which is the heart of a mother.

This is the aspect of the Divine Master that we love to contemplate. We accept our share in these exquisite outpourings, all of us whom He still calls to that intimacy which He allowed His disciples while on earth. We, too, are His friends, His brothers. To us also has He said, "As my Father has loved me, I also love you." By the gift of grace He bestows on us, it is a true fellowship that we have formed with Him. We can call Him our friend, our other self, without failing in respect toward Him, without doing anything less than responding to the dearest desire of His heart. We can converse with Him in spirit, concern ourselves with His interests, inquire into His mysteries, and become preoccupied with the cause of His glory. We have the freedom of the city in Heaven, which is His kingdom now, and ours through Him. "Our life is in Heaven," says St. Paul.[155]

The kindness of Jesus toward His own is manifested, as we have said, by the vocation to which He calls them and by the intimacy to which He leads them. It is evinced once more by His patience.

There was need for patience, with these men — ignorant, rude, full of defects (like all of us) — full of good will, too, but weak, and blind beyond measure. When the tone of the Master's discourse is elevated the least bit, they no longer understand, or they forget almost immediately and return to their

[155] Cf. Phil. 3:20.

nature — rather, let us say simply to nature, period; we know what the nature of man is like.

He preaches humility to them, and they constantly maneuver for the first place; He preaches charity, and they want to call down fire from Heaven on the towns.[156] He wears Himself out trying to make them understand what He is doing, the spiritual character of His work, in contrast to what the Jews were expecting of their Messiah, and they stubbornly cling to the prejudices of their compatriots.

"My kingdom is not of this world,"[157] He says to them continually. "The kingdom of God is within you. . . . Seek not that which perisheth, but that which abideth unto life eternal."[158] These are words frequently on His lips; they resound in the ears of His disciples, but slip over their souls like the seed over a rock, while they insistently pose the question: "When, therefore, wilt Thou re-establish the kingdom of Israel?"[159]

When He instructs them concerning Himself, the future that awaits Him — the Cross instead of the material empire for which they clamor — His confidences, far from enlightening, overwhelm them. There they are, listening, trusting, and struck with incomprehension as if in a dream. "They did not understand what He said to them. . . . Their eyes were held. . . . They were in a stupor."[160] Such expressions recur often on the pens of the Evangelists.

---

[156] Cf. Mark 9:33; Luke 9:54.
[157] John 18:36.
[158] Luke 17:21; John 6:27.
[159] Acts 1:6.
[160] Luke 9:45; cf. Mark 6:51.

After certain particularly disturbing revelations, their hearts are so troubled that they rise as if in a movement of revolt.

No one can forget that incident, so characteristic of their state of soul, in which Simon Peter should have been the hero, the leader giving the cue to the whole group. It was at Caesarea Philippi. Jesus was announcing His Passion and how He was to suffer much at the hands of the elders, the high priests, and the scribes, and to be put to death. And Peter dares to contradict Him: "God forbid, Lord! That will never happen. Let that be far from Thee, Master!" And Jesus, severe in this instance, as He had reason to be, turns around in indignation: "Satan! Depart from me; thou art a scandal to me! Thou understandest nothing of the things of God; thou hast none but human thoughts!"[161] Poor Saint Peter! He must have rejoined the group somewhat shamefacedly; but he knew well the heart from which such words proceeded.

Besides, this was an extremely rare instance. Ordinarily Jesus did not assume this tone with the disciples. He exercised patience. For all their miseries, He had inexhaustible condescension, compassion, forbearance, and the indulgence of a mother. Even their foolishness in no way altered the exquisite sentiments and affections He evinced toward them.

Here is the account that is the necessary corrective of the preceding one, and perhaps among the most delightful in the Gospel, which contains so many beautiful ones.

Jesus was alone. The disciples formed a group some distance away. Doubtless they had just been having one of those discussions about priority that they often held, which witnessed to

[161] Cf. Matt. 16:21-23.

the weakness of these men and to human weakness in general. Then they approached and asked this question of the Master: "Master, which of us is the greatest in the kingdom of Heaven?" As His only reply, Jesus beckoned to a little child who happened to be there; He set him in the midst of them and said, "In very truth, I say to you, he who humbles himself and becomes like unto this little child will be the greatest in the kingdom of Heaven."[162] It is a charming picture, worthy of this Son of God, full of grace and truth,[163] of whom the apostle speaks, and who manifests His indulgence so fittingly!

For it must be admitted, there was something annoying, almost revolting in these constant demands on the part of men who had received everything and who were forever engaged in a stupid quarrel for first place. He recognized this better than anyone; but they were His children just the same; they were the little flock for whom He would give His life. And He put up with them, looked after them, and, not being able or not wishing to transform them right away, He waited for them.

How often God is obliged to wait, when it comes to man! With our insane pride, our nonexistent charity, our outrageous selfishness toward Him from whom we obtain everything, the ruthlessness with which we fall upon anything that flatters us, regardless of duty, regardless of what God might think of it, since He asks us to forget ourselves somewhat for His sake, as He forgot Himself for us, and as He expects someday to forget Himself in us: how often would we not tire out the most long-suffering patience! And God does wait! He

[162] Matt. 18:1-4.
[163] John 1:14.

stands at the door, as He tells us, and knocks.[164] He makes the best of our backwardness; He bides His time to tell us tomorrow what we refuse to listen to today, and, in the face of our coldness and resistance, He continues to shed His grace, as the sun shines, majestic and serene, over the polar ice fields.

That is how Jesus proceeds with His disciples. He operates by His influence, not by reproaches. He knows that God has His hour, that man has his, too; and instead of recrimination, He uses patience; He instructs them and waits for His instruction to sink in. There they are, His own, under His eye; and He lies in wait for an opening within those hearts that gravitate toward Him. Then He enters, lays siege, and sometimes He conquers and sometimes He fails; but always and everywhere, He loves.

Transfer this to the Passion, to those dark days when the soul of the Savior, forced back in every direction from without, seems to retire within itself and lift His sentiments to their highest pitch. How the divine patience manifests itself, then, amid unfathomable expressions of tenderness.

Just consider that discourse on the night before His death, in the upper room where the paschal meal was terminating under the dim light of the lamps, which made the shadows flicker, just as the imminent danger caused all hearts to tremble. And consider the terrifying prophecies that followed, and the abounding consolation of those effusions that only the beloved disciple dared to record, and above all of this, the feelings — truly those of a mother! Consider the desire to comfort them beforehand, in view of the cowardly conduct they will

[164] Rev. 3:20.

be guilty of on the morrow; to excuse them, on His part, for what they are going to do against Him; to forestall maternally, by interposing His tender affection, the crushing blow of remorse upon their hearts. What a scene it is!

"My little children," He said to them, "I am but a little while in the midst of you. You will seek me. And as I said to the Jews, you cannot come now where I am going." And Simon Peter exclaimed, "Lord, why can I not follow You? I will give my life for You." "You will give your life for me? In truth, I tell you, before the cock crows, you will deny me thrice." But He added, "Let not your heart be troubled. You believe in God; believe also in me."[165]

A little later, perceiving their earnestness and burning ardor, quickened by the mounting tide of His affection and the eager outbursts whereby they assured Him of their faith, He said to them, "Do you now believe? Behold, the hour is coming, and has already come, for you to be scattered and to leave me alone! But I am not alone, because the Father is with me. These things I have spoken to you that in me you may have peace."[166]

How admirable is this heart of Christ. Like a mother who, at the departure of the prodigal, thinks only of the danger menacing her child; who, as she watches him stride off in his self-assurance, calculates only the harm he is doing himself while he breaks her heart: so it is with Jesus.

The disciples are not self-assured; but how frightfully weak they are. And He, in His kindness and patience, thinks of

[165] Cf. John 13:33, 37-14:1.
[166] John 16:31-33.

nothing but the discouragement that may overtake them after their fall; so He puts them on their guard: Let not your heart be troubled! When these things come to pass, remember that I told you beforehand and that, in telling you, my whole heart poured forth into yours. Then, instead of crouching there, overwhelmed by your fall, rise up with confidence in me.

We recognize in this the heart of the Master.

But what would we say about it if our name were Judas?

Judas, one of the chosen twelve, one of those to whom Jesus said, "I have not called you servants, but friends":[167] he it is who is to betray his Master — for thirty pieces of silver. And Jesus knew it.[168] For three years, He kept him there among His intimates, treating him like the rest, calling him to the same destiny, and surrounding him with the same delicate attentions. Nothing ever aroused a suspicion — except perhaps in John, where the intuition of love seems to have divined the traitor — a suspicion that He knew whom He had chosen, as He would say.

He even gave Judas a mark of special trust: he was the one who carried the purse belonging to the little band of Apostles. Already he had given evidence of being avaricious; and John had been keen enough to observe it.[169]

As for Jesus, He closed His eyes to it and allowed time and grace to take their course. Before that heart, which was gradually closing itself against Him, He opened up the treasures of His forbearance; He was prodigal of His forgiveness, that rare

---

[167] Cf. John 15:15.
[168] Cf. Matt. 26:15; John 13:11.
[169] John 12:6.

and precious gift which most men are nearly always reluctant to bestow.

What mystery there is in this attitude of Jesus confronted by the traitor. Perhaps nothing enables us to penetrate deeper into that heart than an analysis of what He must have felt then, at every contact.

He was willing to experience at length and in silence that royal sorrow of betrayal — of betrayal by an intimate, by one who has been showered with kindnesses. He had poured them forth upon Judas, knowing all the while that he would show himself a monster. He spoke to him with consideration, with the vision of his crime before Him. He washed his feet on that Thursday evening, conscious that He had already been sold.[170]

And in the garden of Gethsemane, when the miserable man had destroyed the last barrier that still held back the torrent of hatred, of iniquity, and of torture with his infamous kiss, the only revenge of Jesus was the gentle query: "My poor friend, what have you come here to do?"[171] Once more He gave Judas the title of friend, which He had perhaps not applied to him at supper. He wanted him to know he had a right to it, as the final effort put forth by the patience of God.

If the sublimity of kindness is to be found anywhere, it is here; and this ultimate gesture reveals a still vaster horizon upon the sentiments of Jesus toward the Twelve. For this heart, revealed to Judas, He had opened to them all. From that abyss of tenderness they had all drunk, quenching their thirst

[170] John 13:1-5.
[171] Cf. Matt. 26:50.

without appreciating it, but nonetheless really, at the Savior's fountain.

But as if this were not enough, once He had left His own, Jesus willed to give them a last pledge of His bounty. He had called them to a supernal vocation. He had admitted them to an intimacy that was staggering. He had endured everything from them, without allowing it to affect His love. By the gift of His Spirit, He would further complete and apparently terminate the extraordinary work that He had undertaken in these men.

His heart was still not satisfied. To crown it all; to render their vocation even more beautiful; to achieve their intimacy by a perfect resemblance; to remove the very last speck of dust from which His patience must have suffered; finally to add the last jewel to their diadem, the ultimate guarantee to their happiness, the supreme gift to His affection: He gave them what can be given only by omnipotence and perfect love. He gave them the privilege of dying for His sake.[172]

---

[172] According to tradition, all of the Apostles except John were martyred.

Chapter Eight
∞

The World:
He Rejoices in
God's Creation

∞

Nowadays a great deal of attention is paid to our relationship with nature. The close ties of a man with the soil that bore him, whence he sprung forth, so to speak, from which he still daily draws his life until the moment when he returns to it, are a matter of concern as never before. This concern is an important cultural phenomenon.

Unfortunately, our ideas tend toward exaggeration and, with the help of certain prejudices, we have reached the point (under the pretext that nature has an influence upon us) of making nature responsible for all that we are, without any regard for the part played by the will, let alone (since this was more insistently under attack) the more important role of God.

With reference to Jesus Christ, those who obstinately profess to see in Him merely a man are quite naturally inclined to apply this type of thinking to Him. It is noticeable that they lavish their efforts on accommodating descriptions: of Palestine on the one hand, and of the moral personality of Jesus on the other, whence they conclude: the former inevitably produced the latter.

They forget to explain why this Galilee from which the gentle Master came forth was precisely the most turbulent of provinces; why the shores of Tiberias produced, in turn, first

the Sermon on the Mount[173] and then the most narrow-
minded, gloomy, and hateful of rabbinical speculations.

Let us now dwell upon this viewpoint; rather let us gather
up the authentic contacts of Jesus with nature. Let us see what
He owes to it and how He repays this debt.

∞

We have already observed, with regard to the personality
of Jesus and to His preaching, what ought to be attributed to
nature, both in the formation of His humanity and, by an easily comprehensible logic, in the manifestations of this humanity. Nature did not make Jesus what He was; but it contributed
its share in doing so. He proceeds from God, who is His Father,
but He has Mary for His mother. Through Mary, He is the
child of one race, and by way of that race, He is a son of earth,
a son of a particular clime, of a special environment that necessarily had an influence on His humanity, except for the possibility of a miracle, which there is no reason to expect.

No doubt these influences must not be exaggerated. Jesus
was primarily what He willed to be, what He had to be to correspond to the universality of His mission. But there was no
motive for Him to refuse to belong to His race and native land.
Like a plant, which has its own individual species and yet requires something from the soil, whose particular quality rises
and blossoms forth in shape, color, fragrance, and taste, so it is
with Jesus. He draws everything from Himself, in a certain
sense, since there is nothing in Him that He has not willed;
yet He springs from nature, and we have recognized racial

[173] Matt. 5-7.

characteristics and natural influences even in His preaching. However universal it might have been, we have said, and although it was addressed beyond His meager audience to all nations and all ages, it nevertheless possessed what might be called, in the etymological sense of the word, its own *originality*, that is to say, the stamp of its origin, its special flavor, the taste of the soil, if we may be allowed such an expression. Why? Because speech reflects the whole man, and a man always reflects his environment more or less.

Thought does not issue from our intelligence in the abstract. In passing, it borrows from the imagination, which, in turn, draws upon its resources: on the one hand, from the heredity whence it proceeds; on the other, from the surrounding milieu upon which it feeds. The imagination is a kind of reservoir, but a living reservoir, appropriating in its own way, storing up in the course of a lifetime colors, forms, impressions, and memories, feeding our thought with them as they are born in the mind.

This process went on in Jesus as in everyone else. In His case, it was judged, controlled, and ordered, as it is not in us; but it did take place. All His impressions of nature had their use; they were for Him, as for us, always to the extent that He willed it, the milk of the intellect, influencing its external manifestations, as material milk affects the life of the body.

What was the result with regard to the sentiments of Jesus toward nature? The result was that He was more apt than anyone else to understand it and, by understanding, to love it accordingly. What causes us to love nature, in fact, is on the one hand, the sense of beauty we find in it. Moreover, there is a secret harmony between what it is and what we are. Nature has made us, to the extent we have just explained; our powers issue from its powers, and it exerts a constant influence upon our powers. Hence, admiring and loving nature means return-ing to one's source; and the more we have received from it, the more congeniality there is in that return.

Must we not conclude that the feeling for nature in Jesus was necessarily exquisite; that His humanity found there one more path leading to the Father, as well as the occasion of delightful and most intense enjoyment?

It is pleasant also to observe that Jesus was well situated for the appreciation of nature. The spot on earth to which Heaven had descended was one of the most beautiful and richest on this globe. No native land had ever been loved more, and al-though there were manifold reasons for this love — so that it was not from purely aesthetic motives that the prophets had uttered such passionate, grandiloquent outbursts: "Let those who love thee, O Zion, be like the sun when it rises in power"[174] — the appreciation of the beautiful had a large share in such enthusiasm. "The Promised Land" was not a meaning-less term; "the land flowing with milk and honey"[175] was not false advertising. Every Israelite was proud of his fair land.

During the lifetime of Jesus, this land was at the height of its development and productiveness. It did not possess, like the Bosporus or the Grecian isles, an intoxicating charm con-ducive to voluptuous languor; there was about it an expansive, wholesome beauty with a tinge of melancholy. For the oriental sun, combined with the amazing topography of Palestine and

[174] Cf. Judg. 5:31.
[175] Exod. 3:8.

the system of waterways that irrigated it, made of this little country a supremely favored region.

In this clime, as soon as spring appears, the heat begins and nature becomes industrious; all around the edge of the smallest waterhole, a paradise of greenery blossoms forth. The Jordan River traverses the center of Palestine from end to end. In Jesus' day, numerous springs, carefully channeled, distributed their waters throughout the land, and rewarded the labors of man with produce of every variety.

At the bottom of the great valley hollowed out from north to south like a plowed furrow; from the shores of the lake, lying some six hundred and fifty feet below the level of the Mediterranean, down to the Dead Sea, which sinks to seventeen hundred and fifty feet below; to the right and left of the Jordan, sheltered from the violence of the winds, the landscape had the appearance and the vegetation of the tropics.

Each season vied for the possession of the land, according to Josephus.[176] There were countless clusters of palm trees; Solomon's balsams shed their fragrance everywhere; delightfully scented orchards, enjoying abundant irrigation, made of Jericho especially a garden spot famous throughout the country; homes and palaces converged there under the aureole of palms, studding the verdant plane with their dazzling whiteness. And higher up, on the slopes of the hills and the undulating plateaus at the summits, stretched a temperate zone, also lavishly favored, since it continued to produce two crops annually.

Such was the condition of Galilee, Samaria, and western Perea.

[176] Flavius Josephus (c. 37-100), Jewish historian.

But the land of Judah — Judea, properly called — possessed neither this fruitfulness nor its charm. One might have thought that God had intended to establish a distinction between the region that listened to the good tidings and the city of deicide that tried to stifle His voice. The district was mountainous, and water was scarce. There were stony outcroppings everywhere and, here and there, only a thin layer of soil, as if the land were but skin and bones. On the whole, it looked dejected and abandoned. Seeing Jerusalem in the midst of these ashen defiles, one would have said that the enormous mass of Mount Moriah and the walls of the Temple had fallen out of Heaven onto the plain, producing the swells that contorted the landscape as with the convolutions of waves.

The book of Canticles makes use of an expression that vividly portrays this characteristic: "Hark! my lover: here he comes springing across the mountains, leaping across the hills."[177] That is exactly it. Journeys were made there as if by leaps; but they were not on that account devoid of charm. There emanated from that monotonous natural scenery, under a burning sky, the quality of a very lofty, highly spiritualized dream, which apparently must have contributed to the formation, among the poets of Judah, of the supreme bards of the soul, and even in their descriptions of nature, of the immaterial world.

However that may be, Jesus must have reveled, far beyond any other human being, in all the facets of His earthly country's appeal. He loved that soil on which His divine seed had germinated; He was sensitive, in a degree proportionate to the

[177] Cf. Cant. 2:8 (RSV = Song of Sol. 2:8).

very perfection of His human nature, to all that appealed externally to the instinct of beauty present in that nature. He who proclaimed from the shore of the lake, "See the lilies of the field, how they grow,"[178] must have rested His gaze in sheer delight upon that carpet of scarlet anemones springing up everywhere underfoot, arrayed more richly than Solomon in his royal purple. He loved the labors of the field, reference to which recurs so frequently in His parables.[179] He loved the mountains, the waters, the multicolored vegetation with its infinite variety of scents, the glory of the earth, manifesting and symbolizing all together the glory of God. In the course of His journeys, which were certainly undertaken with a purpose beyond that of aesthetic contemplation, He certainly did not deny Himself the liberty of casting a glance about and momentarily resting His heart upon that nature scattering its treasures in His path, as flowers are strewn before our pilgrim God in the processions of the countryside.

∞

Two highroads in particular were frequently used by the Master. They were those then uniting Jerusalem and Galilee, the twofold scene of His apostolic action. It was especially during the most beautiful season that Jesus traversed these routes.

Assuredly, He took to the road in any weather when necessary, even in the torrid heat of midsummer, even in the melting snows and sodden fields of winter. And in fact, there is no more touching picture than that of Jesus in the rain and storm,

[178] Matt. 6:28.
[179] Cf. Matt. 13:3-8, 24-32; Mark 4:3-8, 26-32; Luke 8:5-8.

going after the lost sheep,[180] or parched with thirst as He carries out, with the Samaritan woman at the well,[181] that poignant stanza of the *Dies Irae:*[182] "Didst sit forspent from seeking me." Yet this was not the usual case. At the two extreme seasons, there was a lull in Jewish life; then Jesus traveled little. Hence His journeys ordinarily coincided with the fine weather, especially with the three great feasts that every devout Jew celebrated: the Pasch, Pentecost, and the Feast of Tabernacles.[183]

He journeyed by short stages so as not to interrupt His ministry, stopping on the way in the towns, preaching, healing, joining other pilgrims on the road, profiting by the leisure and tranquillity of time spent in walking so as to penetrate into the souls and touch the hearts of His traveling companions.

Sometimes, setting out from Nazareth or Capernaum, He would plunge into that valley we have already described, skirting the banks of the Jordan overhung with the branches of willows and oleanders and gliding along with a quiet murmur past its chain of hills; calling a halt so as to preach the good news in the numerous villages ranged one above the other on

---

[180] Luke 15:4.

[181] John 4:6-7.

[182] The *Dies Irae*, literally "the day of wrath," is a traditional Latin hymn about Judgment Day.

[183] The Pasch was the Jewish feast of Passover, commemorating the Exodus, and described in Chapter 12 of the book of Exodus. Pentecost, or the Feast of Weeks, which fell on the fiftieth day after Passover, marked the presentation of the first-fruits of the harvest (Deut. 16:9-12). The last and greatest feast of the year, the Feast of Tabernacles, or Booths, was the autumn thanksgiving festival, during which the people dwelled in booths, or tabernacles, to recall the Jews' sojourn in the wilderness (Lev. 23:39-43; Deut. 16:13-15).

the left side, making His way to the next one by following the sunken curves of the valleys that connect them, as if by inverted bridges.

Then, having reached a point not far from the Dead Sea, which stretched out like a shining sword at the feet of the giant of Moab, Jesus would leave the river, pass through Jericho, take a rocky footpath over the famous ascent of *adoummim*, where even today the blood-red soil reminds the visitor of the parable of the Good Samaritan,[184] and after a final stop in Bethany at the home of Lazarus,[185] He would enter Jerusalem by way of Gethsemane.

But most often He took the road through Samaria which was frequented by the greater number and followed by the Galilean pilgrimages at the seasons of the major festivals; it was the one Jesus Himself had taken three times annually for several years, the road on which Mary and Joseph discovered that He was lost when He was twelve years old.[186]

On leaving Nazareth, this road traversed the great plain of Esdrelon, truly the granary of Palestine. In springtime it is naught but one vast sea of waving verdure, in which flowers of every hue form a mosaic of shifting colors; and in this plain is set the inverted bowl of Tabor. Beyond it to the left is Mount Gelboe, with Ender, where Saul came to consult the witch.[187] On the lower slopes of these same hills, protected by a rampart of cactus with its screen of thorns, is the village of Nain, where

---

[184] Luke 10:30-37.

[185] Cf. John 12:1-2.

[186] Luke 2:43-45.

[187] 1 Kings 28:7 (RSV = 1 Sam. 28:7).

Jesus raised to life the widow's son;[188] Shunem, redolent with memories of the prophet Elisha;[189] then En-Gannim with its crown of palms, the region of the ten lepers in the Gospel;[190] and next comes Dothan, where Joseph was sold.[191] The caravans of the Ismaelites still pass along there, with their long lines of camels, en route for Egypt.

Then we reach Samaria, ancient capital of Israel; and Shechem with its lush gardens, its lovely valley, and its temple — perched atop Mount Gerizim, in competition with that of Jerusalem, by the Samaritan schismatics[192] — and the well of Jacob, which it is so hard to leave once we realize that it saw the presence of the Divine Master seated there, and that the vista one contemplates was reflected in His eyes when He said, "See the fields white for the harvest. . . ."[193]

Finally, we come to Shiloh, where the ark rested;[194] Bethel, where the sleeping Jacob caught a glimpse of Heaven;[195] and, having been four days on the way, we arrive at the vantage point of Mount Scopus, whence the panorama of Jerusalem opens out to our gaze.

The rabbis used to say, "God gave the world ten measures of beauty, and nine of them were bestowed upon Jerusalem." It

[188] Luke 7:11-15.

[189] 4 Kings 4:8-37 (RSV = 2 Kings 4:8-37).

[190] Luke 17:12-19.

[191] Gen. 37:28.

[192] Cf. John 4:20.

[193] Cf. John 4:35.

[194] Cf. 1 Kings 4:4 (1 Sam. 4:4).

[195] Cf. Gen. 28:10-19.

was doubtless from this outlook that they formed such a judgment. It would, in fact, be difficult to find a more beautiful setting. Many a time, no doubt, exhausted with His prolonged marches, Jesus must have sat there on some rock and contemplated admiringly yet sadly, as He considered its future, this noble but ill-fated Jerusalem.

Nowadays, when, in memory of the Divine Master, we cross all these paths along which His steps hastened, we are forced to admit that they have lost a great part of their charm. Islamism has covered it with a shroud, as in all the lands where it prevails. The lovely forests have disappeared; the cultivation of the soil is rare; the valleys are a tangle of wild shrubs. Instead of vineyards, fields of grain, and olive groves arranged in terraces — as formerly when, as the psalmist expressed it, "rejoicing clothed the hills," the pastures were "garmented with flocks," and all the earth "shouted and sang for joy"[196] — desolation now reigns everywhere. The aqueducts are demolished, and the countryfolk lie sunken in sloth. The soil, groggy under the sun's rays, sighs in vain for the drop of water that would fructify it and the minimum of labor that would enable it to yield its treasures. Buried under the brambles, overgrown with unproductive vegetation, where the thistles — to mention only this symbol of wrack and ruin — grow taller than a man on horseback, this land, far from being the shout of joy described by the prophet, is but one long, sad call appealing to man, who has abandoned it.

And yet it is still beautiful, this Palestine, we are glad to say; if need be, we would embellish it in thought, as we are

[196] Cf. Ps. 64:13-14 (RSV = Ps. 65:12-13).

inclined to adorn all that is loved. Its broad outlines have not changed. It is not difficult to picture what it was when the Savior passed leisurely through these valleys, climbed these ridges of hills, sometimes in silence and prayer, sometimes conversing with His disciples, letting His eyes absorb the light, soak up the colors, and contemplate the wide, noble expanses, the blend of energy and grace, and that shimmering radiance that makes our northern landscapes, when we return to them, appear quite gray and dark, like steel engravings.

We can imagine how the soul of the Master must have delighted in these spectacles. And we enjoy them together with Him.

Then a strange thing happens: the very desolation becomes a charm. In the course of long stretches where there is nothing to look at but light, colors, and shapes, without any life, anything to distract or relieve the monotony, the dream becomes more intense. The soul's gaze becomes more practiced. The majesty of the solitudes takes possession of us. The awesome silence penetrates like an all-pervasive fluid. There is a confused murmur in the atmosphere, falling from the hilltops, rising from the ground, where the hoofbeats of the horses produce a strange resonance, driving toward us gusts of memories that gradually take possession of us, invade our soul completely, and set aringing countless dream voices from the past.

Then, not infrequently, under that torrid heat, the conscious mind falls to slumbering. We go along as if drawn by an unknown power, as if confined within a tenuous network of invisible meshes. Letting our miserable personality melt away and vanish into nothingness, we strive to live the Master's life,

seeing with our eyes, beyond the slackened web of things present, the ideal richness of the past.

∞

We cannot be satisfied with stopping here with regard to
the attitude of Jesus toward nature. It would be a childish mistake to imagine that He could have looked upon it solely as an
artist. Even to us, art is no more than a sublime diversion. It is
a pure, lofty form of joy; but it is an idle joy if it never goes beyond itself. To possess any value, it must rise above its earthly
object and, beyond the mirror of creatures, follow the ray of
light that terminates in its primary source, which is God.

This is what Jesus Christ achieved. A threefold homage
rose from His soul toward God when He looked upon nature.
As the Creator of nature, He hailed it, His creation. His
thoughts went back through the centuries to that first day,
when everything came forth from the mind of God; when every being, however infinitesimal, received its name from that
voice which confers existence upon things, whereby each
creature, tiny as it may be, is blessed.

Rather let us say that without any need of going back into
the past, He saw in the present itself every creature dependent
upon God, all life drawing its sustenance from this source, all
activity proceeding from Him, all existence enkindled by
Him, all richness derived from His, all of nature as an emana-
tion, a breath from the divine mouth.

In fact, such is indeed the eternal order of things. God
alone exists by Himself. When He utters His name, He proves
His right to live, for He is Being. But all others, possessed of
only a restricted being, have but a borrowed existence; they

depend upon the first Being. As the ray depends upon the sun at every instant, since the sun is its source and the very center of its life, so is it with us; so is it with nature.

Jesus Christ saw things in this light. After having pursued this contemplation from God down to earth, He put it into reverse, so to speak, by going from the earth back to God. He followed the ray from the mirror to the object, from the creature to the Divine. As a matter of fact, God is not only the Creator of things, He is also their prototype. No beauty would have any charm for us, were it not a reflection of His beauty; no grandeur would impress us, if it were not the image of His grandeur.

God! It is He whom all the voices and all the echoes of this world proclaim. Every age, every being, every creation, every life: all stammer in unison that name which the Hebrews did not dare to pronounce. Each being speaks one syllable of it. The light has its own; the darkness another — those oriental nights which Jesus loved, under cover of which He began His nocturnal prayer; those mild, luminous hours whose poignant majesty must have harmonized so well with the state of His soul, for He discerned therein the tranquil glory of the heavenly Father, His gaze brooding over the earth to keep watch and ward. From top to bottom of the scale of being, from the immensities even to the microscopic, equally unfathomable in the abysses toward which they recede, everything sang to Him of God, declared His glory, and proclaimed as great, beautiful, and magnificent the Creator of the universe.

But here we find another mystery. He of whom we speak, Jesus Christ, is indeed God; but not simply God: He is the God who is Wisdom, the God who is Beauty, the God who mirrors the perfections of the Father; "the image of His substance,"[197] St. Paul calls Him; His Word or Utterance, says St. John:[198] the interior, living word, expressing to God all that He thinks and all that He is.

It is therefore Jesus Christ, considered as the second Person of the Trinity, who is the universal exemplar, the prototype of creatures, the substantial idea, who embraces all, in whom consequently the plan of the world subsists.

Thus, by a mystery that overwhelms us (is there anything in Him that is not mystery?), Jesus Christ combines in Himself — God and Man — admiration for nature and authority over nature. He looks upon it, and He produces it; He is the model, and He rejoices in the resemblance. He perceives nature with a twofold gaze: one cast upon the exterior, the copy, which is necessarily faulty; the other concentrated within on the original concept, which is the creative thought, which is Himself, which is God.

Finally, just as He saw all things coming forth from God, reflecting God, so did He also see all things returning to God. Creation is a circle. God produces; His work evolves under the empire of the laws He determines for it. It seeks out its path amid gropings and obstacles; then, having described a vast circuit, it necessarily returns to its source.

All things work for the Creator. Everything should find its consummation in Him, with the tranquillity of a definitive, immutable structure. Now, Jesus saw this future in the process of accomplishment. He saw in nature God's workman; the

[197] Cf. Col. 1:15.
[198] John 1:1.

mysterious artisan of a still more mysterious product, but one that God comprehends and directs. "Man bestirs himself; God propels him," said Fénelon;[199] nature, too, bestirs itself, and God controls it. As that power, gentle but irresistible, which drives through space the dizzily speeding, placid stars: that was how Jesus looked on Providence. He united Himself to it; He recognized His part in bringing the work to conclusion, just as St. Paul describes it in a sublime vision: all things subject to the elect, the elect subject to Christ, and Christ subject to God[200] — and that eternally.

That is what Jesus discerned in nature. And these awe-inspiring conceptions followed Him everywhere. In the least details of His daily life, they constituted His strength. Can we imagine Jesus Christ, great-souled as He was, taking an interest in the insignificant details that surrounded Him, had He not incorporated them into the immensity that was worthy of Him? But such was the case, and in the course of that poor, squalid existence, that was what sustained Him; in His sufferings, that was His joy.

He willed, too, that it should be the joy of His disciples and ours. "How blind," He said one day, "are you men of little faith. Why are you troubled by the things that happen to you? Two sparrows are sold for a farthing, and I assure you in truth that not one of them falls from the rooftop without the consent of your heavenly Father. Are you not worth much more than sparrows?"[201]

---

[199] François Fénelon (1651-1715), Archbishop of Cambrai.

[200] Cf. 1 Cor. 3:22-23.

[201] Cf. Matt. 10:29, 31.

As can be seen, His concept of nature was transformed into tenderness, to the advantage of man. Instead of the disturbed pessimism of which our century is fond — that sinister, poisonous extract that modern poets draw forth from majestic panoramas, so that the soul shrinks rather than expands — Jesus steeped His followers in divine serenity. He caused them to watch for the currents favorable to creation. The earth at the service of man, his slave even when it makes him suffer; all of nature collaborating with Heaven to bring about the result we are awaiting: that was His message to His disciples. And He inspired them to transmit it to us. Is this not, in fact, the basis of their teaching, the foundation of Christian doctrine? We came from God; all of nature proceeds from Him; out of nature and ourselves, we must reascend to God.

We are the image of God; nature is His footprint. We must contemplate and pay Him homage in all things. We are on the way back to God; the sheerest veil separates us from Him, and death is preparing to tear it asunder. Let us keep ourselves in readiness, and, instead of allowing our life to proceed helter-skelter, without any control or tenacity of purpose, let us set it firmly in the path traced out by the Master.

Let us follow the direction in which all things are tending, but not unconsciously, as in the case of lower nature; not rebelliously — sometimes we are rebels, and that is our great mistake — for God's intent will prevail, regardless. But it can prevail against us! Let us act in such a way that God's will may be accomplished in us and for us, and that we may be happy to be advancing toward our Father and to be fulfilling His will.

∞

Biographical Note

Antonin Gilbert Sertillanges
(1863-1948)

∞

Born in the French city of Clermont-Ferrand on November 16, 1863, A. G. Sertillanges entered the Dominican order twenty years later, taking the religious name Dalmatius. In 1888 he was ordained a priest.

After completing his studies and teaching for a few years, Fr. Sertillanges was appointed secretary of the prestigious scholarly journal *Revue Thomiste*. In 1900 he became professor of moral theology at the Catholic Institute in Paris, where he taught for twenty years. Later, Fr. Sertillanges taught elsewhere in France and also in Holland. During his year-long stay in Jerusalem in 1923, he was inspired to write his acclaimed book *What Jesus Saw from the Cross* (published by Sophia Institute Press in 1996).

His classic book *The Intellectual Life* explains the methods, conditions, habits, and virtues that are necessary in the intellectual life. These virtues bore great fruit in Fr. Sertillanges' own life, enabling him to become a widely recognized expert in the philosophy of St. Thomas Aquinas and to write many books and more than a thousand articles in the areas of philosophy, theology, spirituality, and art.

But Fr. Sertillanges was far more than a professor and scholar. During his lifetime, he was widely admired for his skill as a preacher, a spiritual director, and an apologist, and he was particularly successful in presenting the Faith in compelling terms to the young and to the unconverted.

No "ivory tower" intellectual, but first and foremost a passionate son of the Church, Fr. Sertillanges wrote numerous works that bridge the gap between academic theology and the everyday faith of the ordinary layman.

The fruit of both hard study and devout prayer, and written with the desire to preach Catholic truth *usque ad mortem* ("unto death," in the words of the Dominican motto), the works of Fr. Sertillanges are now informing and inspiring yet another generation of readers in these times of theological uncertainty and moral disarray.

∞

Sophia Institute Press®

Sophia Institute is a nonprofit institution that seeks to restore man's knowledge of eternal truth, including man's knowledge of his own nature, his relation to other persons, and his relation to God.

Sophia Institute Press® serves this end in numerous ways. It publishes translations of foreign works to make them accessible to English-speaking readers. It brings out-of-print books back into print. And it publishes important new books that fulfill the ideals of Sophia Institute. These books afford readers a rich source of the enduring wisdom of mankind. Sophia Institute Press® makes these high-quality books available to the general public by using advanced technology and by soliciting donations to subsidize its general publishing costs.

Your generosity can help Sophia Institute Press® to provide the public with editions of works containing the enduring wisdom of the ages. Please send your tax-deductible contribution to the address below. Your questions, comments, and suggestions are also welcome.

For your free catalog, call:
Toll-free: 1-800-888-9344

or write:
Sophia Institute Press®
Box 5284, Manchester, NH 03108

www.sophiainstitute.com